G000270956

© Haynes Publishing, 2010

The right of Paul Joannou to be identified as the author of this Work has been asserted
by him in accordance with the Copyright, Designs & Patents Act 1988.

All rights reserved. No part of this publication may be reproduced, stored in a retrieval system
or transmitted, in any form or by any means, electronic, mechanical, photocopying, recording
or otherwise, without prior permission in writing from the publisher.

First published in 2010

A catalogue record for this book is available from the British Library

ISBN: 978-1-844259-52-6

Published by Haynes Publishing, Sparkford, Yeovil,
Somerset BA22 7JJ, UK
Tel: 01963 442030 Fax: 01963 440001
Int. tel: +44 1963 442030 Int. fax: +44 1963 440001
E-mail: sales@haynes.co.uk
Website: www.haynes.co.uk

Haynes North America Inc., 861 Lawrence Drive,
Newbury Park, California 91320, USA

All images © Mirrorpix

Creative Director: Kevin Gardner
Packaged for Haynes by BrainWave

Printed and bound in the US

When
FOOTBALL *Was* FOOTBALL

NEWCASTLE UNITED

A Nostalgic Look at a Century of the Club

Paul Joannou

Contents

> *Newcastle United's history is a quite remarkable one – full of incident and drama.*
>
> Sir Bobby Robson

Introduction

When Football Was Football... those were the days! On Tyneside they used to shout at the pit-head: "Any good footballers down there?" It's now all a bit different in the multi-millionaire world of football.

Having arrived for the first time at St James' Park in 1971 after signing for Newcastle United, the great Jackie Milburn met me and said: "Come on, son. I'm taking you house-hunting!"

Nearing Bedlington he turned left at the Ashington sign and explained we were now heading for his hometown and a couple of miles short of there his arm suddenly went across the front of my face as he pointed out of the passenger window.

"Come on now, you soft Southerner," challenged Jackie, "What's that?", as my eyes followed his horizontal finger to an Eiffel Tower type metal structure with a wheel at the top.

"I think, Jackie, it's called a pit-wheel, but I can't be sure", I stammered.

"Maybe you're not so soft after all. But, it's not any old pit-wheel is that. That's the pit-wheel under which I worked as a lad after leaving school, a mile underground all week, never seeing the sun shine.

"But God was good to me, he gave me a rare ability to play football, and like you, pace to burn. Newcastle United offered me a professional contract and I never looked back. But all my schoolmates and family are still there, a mile underground earning the crust to feed their families.

"It's a hard, thankless and unforgiving way to earn a living. So when the weekend comes you'll see them streaming from underground, washing the black from their bodies, and getting on the buses heading for Newcastle where they'll have a pint before making their way to their beloved St James' Park.

"An hour before kick-off they'll be singing their hearts out on the terraces to set the atmosphere for when their team enters from the tunnel.

"This is your only opportunity to repay them for their loyalty and support, for they will never let you down. So from that first whistle you have to set your sights on getting to the penalty area as often as you can. You have to keep taking on defenders, no matter how hard they try to stop you, you must get beyond them and rain as many shots at goal as you can.

"Make the goalkeeper work like he's never worked before. Be relentless in raining those shots down.

"Those goals will start to come, and the more you score the greedier you must become, because those that don't see the daylight until Saturday expect nothing less. There you see, it's easy lad, isn't it?"

Well, no Jackie. It isn't easy, and it never has been, not by a long stretch of the imagination. But it does serve as a great lesson and inspiration. Despite the fact the mines have all but disappeared in the North East and the footballer conveyor-belt of talent from those very pits has long-ended, the indomitable spirit hasn't, and never will.

Malcolm Macdonald

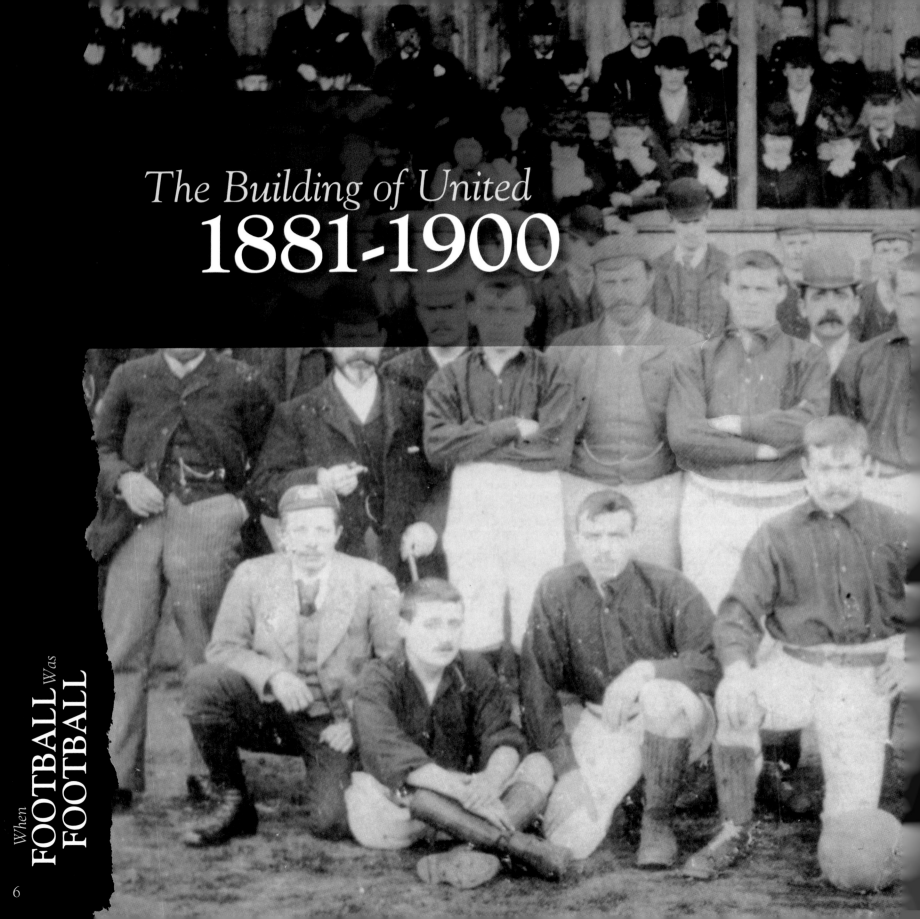

The Building of United
1881-1900

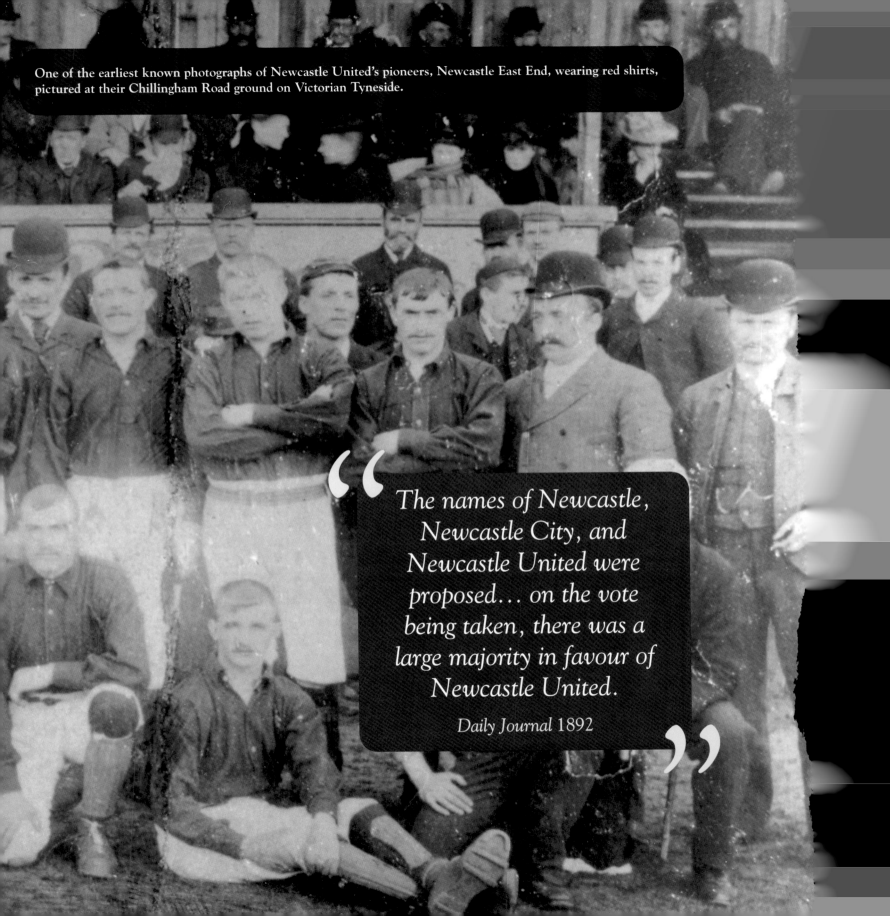

One of the earliest known photographs of Newcastle United's pioneers, Newcastle East End, wearing red shirts, pictured at their Chillingham Road ground on Victorian Tyneside.

> " *The names of Newcastle, Newcastle City, and Newcastle United were proposed… on the vote being taken, there was a large majority in favour of Newcastle United.*
>
> Daily Journal 1892 "

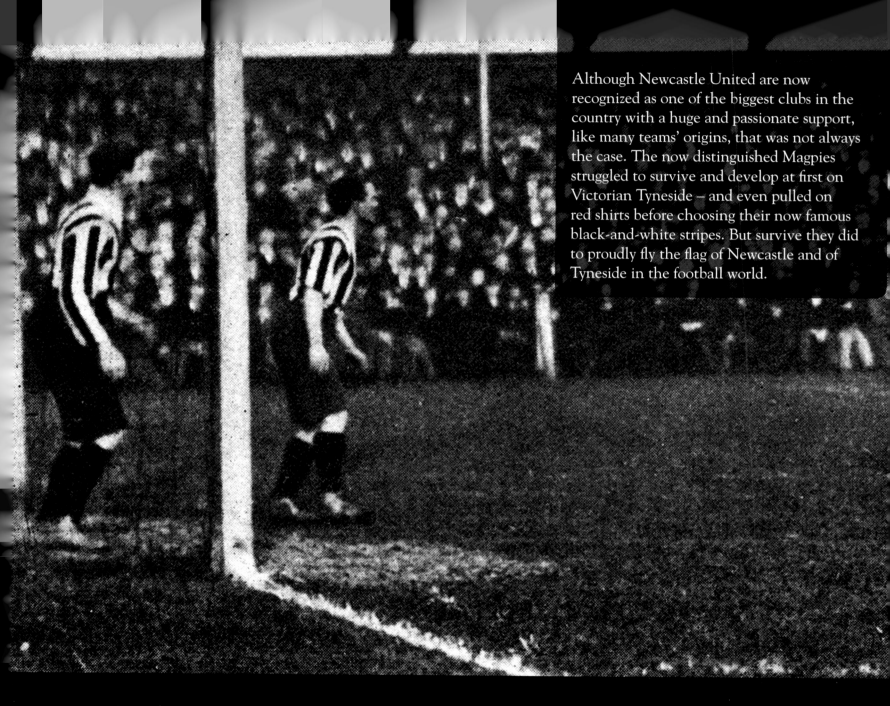

Although Newcastle United are now recognized as one of the biggest clubs in the country with a huge and passionate support, like many teams' origins, that was not always the case. The now distinguished Magpies struggled to survive and develop at first on Victorian Tyneside – and even pulled on red shirts before choosing their now famous black-and-white stripes. But survive they did to proudly fly the flag of Newcastle and of Tyneside in the football world.

1881 Stanley FC formed in the St Peter's area of Byker. **1882** Newcastle West End founded, while Stanley change their name to East End. **1886** West End move to St James' Park. **1887** East End take part in the FA Cup for the first time. **1889** East End and West End both turn professional. **1890** East End and West End both become limited companies. **1892** West End fold due to financial problems and East End take over St James' Park. **1893** East End change their name to Newcastle United and are

Early action at the turn of the century against Nottingham Forest as United defend their goal in numbers. Note the goalkeeper (pictured, between the posts) wears the same shirt as his outfield colleagues and the referee is in civvies clothing.

elected to the Football League. **1894** United change their colours from red shirts to black-and-white stripes. **1895** United lose 0-9 to Burton Wand and 1-7 to Villa in League and FA Cup, both records. **1898** Newcastle win promotion to the top level of football after a series of test matches. **1899** The Magpies complete their first season

Pioneers

Newcastle United owe their origins to a pioneer club located in the city's East End, at St Peter's alongside the River Tyne. Stanley FC were formed in November 1881 from a cricket club of the same name – taken from a local street in the St Peter's and Byker area. In 1882 they changed their name to East End FC and soon made their base at Chillingham Road on the Byker and Heaton border. During the 1880s they developed an intense rivalry with the city's other principal club, Newcastle West End, and by the summer of 1892 they had won their battle for supremacy when the West Enders folded. East End took over their rivals ground at St James' Park, close to the city centre and were set for a headlining future.

United... We Stand

Following the move to St James' Park and the demise of the West End club, the East Enders needed to unify the footballing public on Tyneside. A change of name was the answer, and in December 1892 a public meeting took place in the Bath Lane Hall near to St James' Park to discuss possible new titles for the club. Several names were considered: Newcastle Rangers, Newcastle City, even Newcastle Central or the City of Newcastle. The majority, however, wanted "Newcastle United" – a fitting title. The new United joined the Football League for the 1893/4 season.

ABOVE: As football arrived on Tyneside the Victorian Industrial Revolution had seen the region go through vast expansion and huge change. Trams carried the population around the capital of the North. Pictured here is a tramcar at the turn of the century en route from Central Station to Osborne Road.

LEFT: Club Secretary Frank Watt pictured at his desk at St James' Park. The Scot was a hugely influential figure in shaping Newcastle United into one of the country's finest clubs.

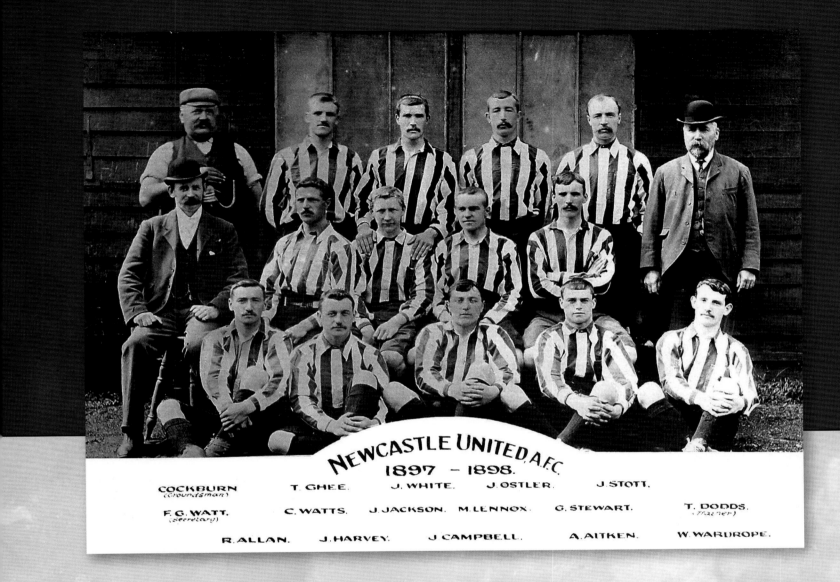

NEWCASTLE UNITED A.F.C.
1897 – 1898.

COCKBURN (Groundsman)   T. GHEE.   J. WHITE.   J. OSTLER.   J. STOTT.

F.G. WATT. (Secretary)   C. WATTS.   J. JACKSON.   M. LENNOX.   G. STEWART.   T. DODDS. (Trainer)

R. ALLAN.   J. HARVEY.   J CAMPBELL.   A. AITKEN.   W. WARDROPE.

Promotion 1898

Newcastle United's development moved apace once they were promoted from the Second Division in the 1897/8 season. Their elevation to the top level of football came through a test match mini-league contest, similar to the play-offs of the present day. In typical United style though, they made it by way of controversy, after bitter complaints of how the test matches were played out. Although they finished out of the winning places, there was much ill feeling when rivals Stoke and Burnley contrived a goalless draw. The test match system was scrapped and Division One extended, allowing Newcastle's entry.

Record:	P30 W21 D3 L6 F64 A32 – 45 Pts – Position 2nd.
Regular side:	Watts, White, Jackson, Ghee, Ostler, Stott, Allen (R), Harvie, Peddie or Campbell, Aitken, Wardrope.
Top scorers:	Peddie 16, Wardrope 10.
Captain:	Jimmy Stott.
Manager:	Director's Committee.

ABOVE: United's successful squad of players and officials reached football's top tier for the first time in 1898. By then they were well and truly in black-and-white stripes.

11

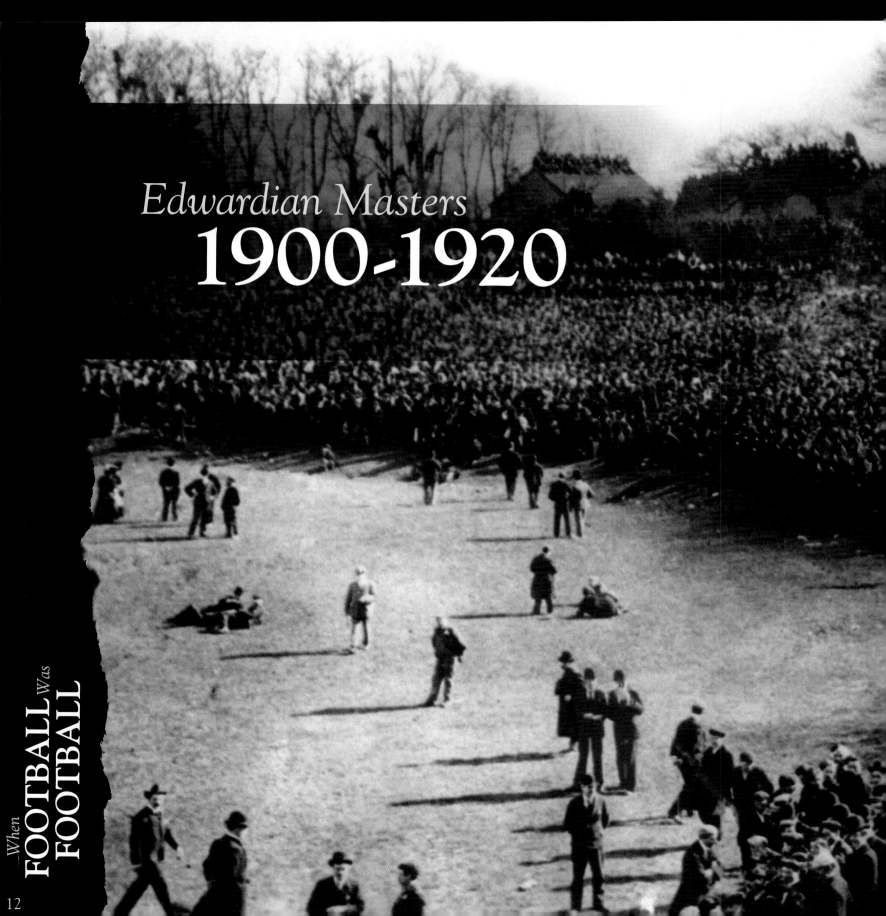

Edwardian Masters
1900-1920

Part of the vast crowd of 101,117 that watched United's first FA Cup final in 1905. The attendance at the old Crystal Palace arena is the biggest to gather at any United fixture.

" *The Newcastle team of the 1900s would give any modern side a two-goal start and beat them, and furthermore, beat them at a trot.* "

Peter McWilliam

1900 First match against a foreign team during the season; a victory over the Kaffirs. **1901** The year of the notorious Good Friday riot before a match with Sunderland. **1902** United complete the season in 3rd spot, their highest placing so far. **1903** Newcastle reach the top of the table for the first time after a great start to the season. **1904** The club embark on their first continental tour, travelling to Denmark. **1905** United are crowned Champions for the first time, but lose the FA Cup final to Villa. **1906** A return to the FA Cup final, but once more a defeat, this time to Everton. **1907** The Black 'n' Whites lift the Football League title again. **1908** United's third FA Cup final in four years ends in another defeat, falling to Wolves. **1909** Newcastle walk away with their third Championship victory in five years. **1910** At last the FA Cup is secured, following a replay against Barnsley. **1911** Another FA Cup final defeat, this time in a replay at the hands of Bradford City. **1912** United challenge for the title again, but finish in 3rd place. **1913** A monumental three-game epic in the FA Cup with Sunderland ends in defeat. **1914** A mid-table position as United's Edwardian mastery comes to a close. **1915** The First World War brings a halt to football; Newcastle all but close down. **1919** Newcastle compete in the Northern Victory League as the game prepares for a restart.

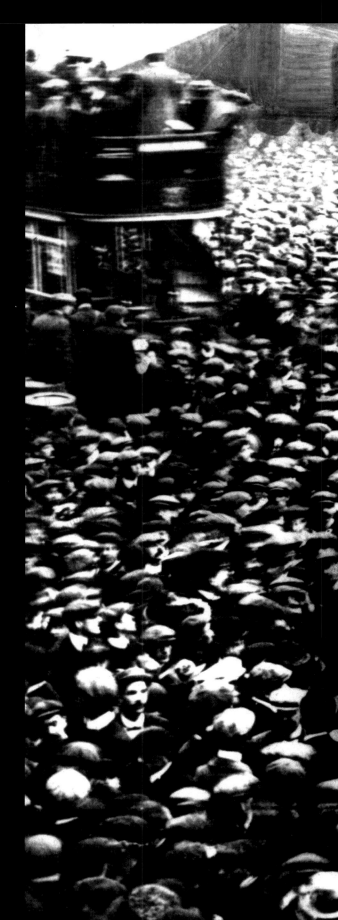

After several attempts during the Edwardian era, the Black 'n' Whites eventually lifted the FA Cup in 1910 and thousands massed on the streets of Tyneside to welcome the team home. United's victory parade passes the Central Station.

Throughout football's history a handful of clubs have dominated an era: four special teams of note are Huddersfield Town during the Twenties, Arsenal in the Thirties, and in more recent times, Manchester United and Liverpool. It was Newcastle United who did the same during the Edwardian period, with its side full of international talent and rank of the very best in the business. They won Football League and FA Cup silverware, and they did it in a manner that pleased almost everyone, with an attractive passing style of football.

AN EXCITING MOMENT IN THE GREAT MATCH FOR THE FOOTBALL CUP.

An attack on the Newcastle United goal during the match for the Football Association Cup, which was witnessed by over 100,000 people at the Crystal Palace on Saturday. Hall, the Aston Villa left wing forward, makes a splendid centre from a corner conceded by Newcastle United, and Brawn nearly succeeds in scoring. Other photographs of the game appear on page 9.—(Russell.)

JUDGE GRANTHAM ON A HAY CART

Mr. Justice Grantham judging the Bar Point-to-point Races, which were held at North Weald on Saturday, from a hay-cart.

TERRIBLE DISASTER WHICH CAUSED EIGHTY DEATHS NEAR MADRID.

Over four hundred workmen were overwhelmed by the bursting of a reservoir near Madrid, and eighty were killed. This photograph, taken just after the disaster, shows the work of rescue still in progress.

THE GREAT MATCH FOR THE FOOTBALL CUP AT THE CRYSTAL PALACE—ASTON VILLA KICK OFF.

The opening of the great match for the Cup at the Crystal Palace, which was witnessed by over 100,000 people—Hampton kicking off for Aston Villa. The small photographs show Spencer, the Aston Villa captain (on the left), a group of enthusiasts in the crowd (in the centre), and Aitken, the Newcastle United captain.—(Photographs by Russell, Whitlock and Thomson and Lee.)

COME FROM UNDER THE SEA TO WATCH THE MATCH.

Rev. P. Parmister, who is leaning on the front wheel of the brake, brought a party of miners from Whitehaven, Cumberland, where their work in a mine that runs out under the sea for miles, to London to see the match.

ASTON VILLA TEAM TAKE A TRIP ON THE THAMES.

While waiting for Saturday afternoon's great ordeal, the Aston Villa team and some of their supporters passed the time by taking a trip on the Thames in a specially-chartered steamer.

ABOVE: How the *Daily Mirror* reported the 1905 FA Cup final between United and Aston Villa in front of a huge attendance at Sydenham. One picture (bottom left) shows a party of miners from Whitehaven that travelled the long journey south by horse-drawn brake!

Off to the Palace

Before the construction of Wembley Stadium in 1923, high-profile fixtures such as FA Cup finals and internationals were for a lengthy period played at the Crystal Palace arena in the capital's suburb of Sydenham. Within a vast parkland dominated by the Victorian Crystal Palace itself – constructed on Sydenham Hill in 1854 – two sporting arenas could be found alongside the fountains and boating lakes. The south ground was used principally for FA Cup finals from 1894 to 1914 and the trip to the Palace became noted as a great day out for travelling supporters, many spending the whole day in the park, having picnics and fun as well as games prior to the main event – the football. Few Geordies of the Edwardian era travelled far in those days, and even fewer to London, so United's five visits to the capital became a highlight of the year for many.

League Champions 1905

Record:	P34 W23 D2 L9 F72 A33 – 48 Pts.
Regular side:	Lawrence, McCombie, Carr, Gardner, Aitken, McWilliam, Rutherford, Howie, Appleyard, Orr or Veitch, Gosnell.
Top scorers:	Howie 14, Appleyard 13.
Captain:	Andy Aitken.
Manager:	Director's Committee.

Having a relatively modest previous campaign, United's first championship victory was a surprise to almost everyone. Indeed, the Magpies nearly carried off the double, also reaching the FA Cup final. The line-up clicked as the New Year approached, the club winning seven games in a row. Their passing and possession style now had the required impact: it was a method of play to become celebrated over the coming years. The Magpies won the title race with Everton and Manchester City by winning their final two games of the season, both away from Tyneside, against Sheffield Wednesday and Middlesbrough.

RIGHT: United's Edwardian side pictured in London before the FA Cup final posed in team formation (3-3-5), and no doubt in their Cup final suits. Back row, left to right: McCombie, Lawrence, Carr. Middle, standing: John Oliver (director), Frank Watt (secretary), Gardner, Aitken, McWilliam, James McPherson (trainer), John Graham (director). Sitting: Rutherford, Howie, Appleyard, Veitch, Gosnell.

FA Cup Final 1905

United's first appearance in the FA Cup final was not a victorious one as they slumped to a two-goal defeat at the hands of the team they were to replace as England's finest, Aston Villa. Although United had beaten Villa home and away in league action, Newcastle never really recovered from a very early goal by man-of-the-match, Villa striker Harry Hampton. The Magpies were criticized for being too cautious and defensive, while the defeat also halted the club's bid of securing the double; but it did reinforce the belief that the Tynesiders had put together a side that would be at the forefront of the English game for a decade.

Date & venue:	15th April 1905 at Crystal Palace. Newcastle United 0(0) Aston Villa 2(1).
United:	Lawrence, McCombie, Carr, Gardner, Aitken, McWilliam, Rutherford, Howie, Appleyard, Veitch, Gosnell.
Villa:	George, Spencer, Miles, Pearson, Leake, Windmill, Brown, Garratty, Hampton, Bache, Hall.
Goals:	Villa – Hampton (2m, 76m).
Attendance:	101,117.
Captain:	Andy Aitken.
Manager:	Director's Committee.

FA Cup Final 1906

United's second final in a row saw them face arch rivals of that era, Everton. Newcastle's league form again deserted them in the showpiece event. The Magpies just could not get going in a contest that was far from being the special occasion all had hoped for. Indeed, the final was a dull and lifeless affair between what were the country's two best sides. The winning goal came when England winger Sharp rounded two United defenders to set up Sandy Young to net.

Date & venue: 21st April 1906 at the Crystal Palace.
Newcastle United 0(0)
Everton 1(0).

United: Lawrence, McCombie, Carr, Gardner, Aitken, McWilliam, Rutherford, Howie, Veitch, Orr, Gosnell.

Everton: Scott, Balmer, Crelley, Makepeace, Taylor, Abbott, Sharp, Bolton, Young, Settle, Hardman.

Goals: Everton – Young (77m).
Attendance: 75,609.
Captain: Alec Gardner.
Manager: Director's Committee.

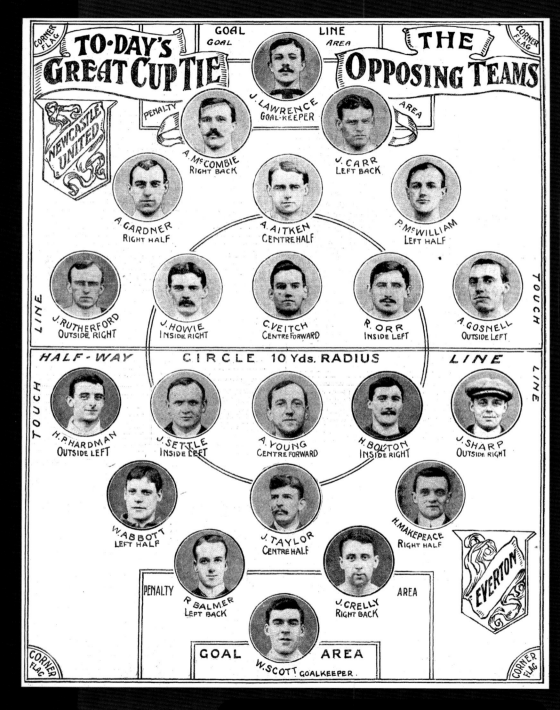

ABOVE: The team line-up featured in the *Daily Mirror* before the 1906 FA Cup final with Everton.

League Champions 1907

United secured their second championship thanks largely to an unbeaten home record which saw the Magpies drop only one point, that against Sheffield United in the match which actually won them the title trophy. They won 18 games on home soil in a row to create a new club record. Sheffield United and Everton were contenders for a period, but it was Bristol City who pushed the Tynesiders most. And an Easter clash between the pair saw the Magpies win 3-0 to all but secure the trophy.

Record:	P38 W22 D7 L9 F74 A46 – 51 Pts.
Regular side:	Lawrence, McCombie or McCracken, Carr, Gardner, Veitch, McWilliam, Rutherford, Howie, Appleyard or Speedie, Orr or Brown, Gosnell.
Top scorers:	Appleyard 17, Rutherford 10.
Captain:	Alec Gardner.
Manager:	Director's Committee.

A superbly arranged photograph of United's squad and officials at the height of their Edwardian Mastery in 1907. The trophies on show are the Football League title and the Sheriff of London Charity Shield, the forerunner of the FA Charity – now Community – Shield.

FA Cup Final 1908

Against Second Division Wolves, United were hot favourites to be victorious at the third attempt in the FA Cup final. But again they never performed to their high standards at the Sydenham arena in London. United gambled by playing Pudan and McWilliam – both struggling with injury – and playmaker Peter McWilliam never got into the game. Yet Newcastle should have been comfortably ahead had England winger Jackie Rutherford not missed two early chances that he would normally have put away. Wolves converted their opportunities to ensure a Cup final shock was recorded.

Date & venue:	25th April 1908 at the Crystal Palace. Newcastle United 1(0) Wolverhampton Wanderers 3(2).
United:	Lawrence, McCracken, Pudan, Gardner, Veitch, McWilliam, Rutherford, Howie, Appleyard, Speedie, Wilson.
Wolves:	Lunn, Jones, Collins, Hunt, Wooldridge, Bishop, Harrison, Shelton, Hedley, Radford, Pedley.
Goals:	United – Howie (73m). Wolves – Hunt (40m), Hedley (43m), Harrison (85m).
Attendance:	74,967.
Captain:	Alec Gardner.

—LEGENDS—

Masters 1

They had the greatest side that was ever, in my opinion, possessed by any club.

Billy Meredith

Newcastle's Edwardian Masters side were a special group of players who took the black and whites to three Football League titles and to five FA Cup finals, once as winners, all in the space of seven seasons.

Colin Veitch: born Newcastle, England international; versatile half-back, the tactical brains of the side.

Andy Aitken: born Ayr, Scottish international; a central midfielder of the highest quality.

Jack Rutherford: born Percy Main, England international; a threat on the right flank at making and taking chances.

Jimmy Lawrence: born Glasgow, Scotland international; consistent in goal, United's record appearance holder.

Jimmy Howie: born Galston, Scotland international; as inside-forward, a genius at creating openings.

Andy McCombie: born Inverness, Scotland international; a rare defender who allied brawn with brains.

Peter McWilliam: born Inveravon, Scotland international; provided vision and quality in midfield.

Bill Appleyard: born Caistor; big and powerful at centre-forward and a handful for any defence.

Alec Gardner: born Leith; a regular in midfield for a decade, the best uncapped player in the country.

Jack Carr: born Seaton Burn, England international; a solid and dependable full-back, rugged at the back.

United's Scottish goalkeeper Jimmy Lawrence who appeared over 14 seasons and totalled a record 496 senior appearances for the club.

–LEGENDS–

Masters 2

Each one of the Edwardian Masters were well known throughout football, respected performers, the majority being international players, several to skipper both club and country during the era.

Albert Shepherd: born Great Lever, England international; a dynamic and crowd-inspiring centre-forward.
Bill McCracken: born Belfast, Ireland international; a maestro in defence who forced a change in the laws.
Ronald Orr: born Bartonholm, Scotland international; small and chunky, with a power-packed shot.
Bert Gosnell: born Colchester, England international; effective on the left wing with consistent approach play.
George Wilson: born Lochgelly, Scotland international; small, fast and tricky, a match-winner on the flank.
Finlay Speedie: born Dumbarton, Scotland international; versatile in all areas of midfield and attack.
Sandy Higgins: born Kilmarnock, Scotland international; possessed a great left foot, a danger up front.
James Stewart: born Gateshead, England international; had a repertoire of delicate skills on the ball.
Wilf Low: born Aberdeen, Scotland international; the enforcer in the midfield battleground.
Tony Whitson: born Cape Town; one of the unsung heroes, a reliable and tough left-back.

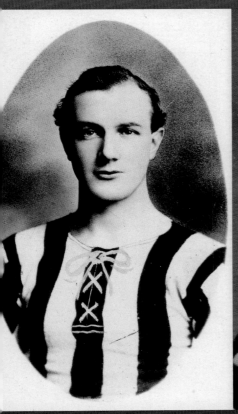
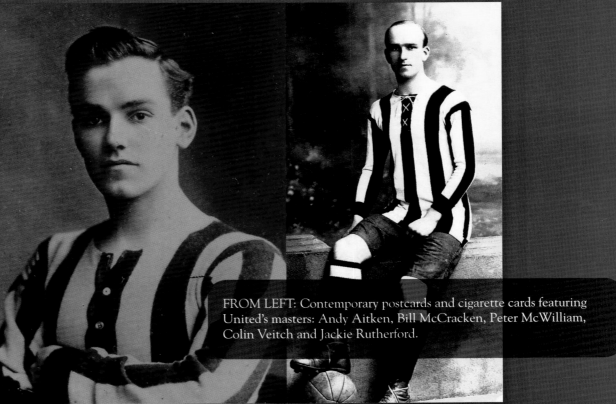

FROM LEFT: Contemporary postcards and cigarette cards featuring United's masters: Andy Aitken, Bill McCracken, Peter McWilliam, Colin Veitch and Jackie Rutherford.

League Champions 1909

Newcastle remarkably still lifted the championship trophy after a headlining and, what still is a record home defeat, 9-1, at the hands of great local rivals Sunderland during December. Never before or since have the Champions elect lost so heavily on their own ground. Yet, amazingly, that point of controversy when a player dispute rocked the club saw United's stars return and cruise to the title creating a new league record points haul. Remaining undefeated for 16 league and Cup games, they saw off a challenge from Everton, winning what was a virtually title decider against the Goodison club by 3-0.

Record: P38 W24 D5 L9 F65 A41 – 53 Pts.

Regular side: Lawrence, McCracken, Whitson, Willis, Veitch, McWilliam, Rutherford, Howie, Shepherd or Higgins, Stewart, Wilson.

Top scorers: Shepherd 11, Veitch 9.

Captain: Colin Veitch.

Manager: Director's Committee.

VOUCHER

THE MORNING JOURNAL WITH THE SECOND LARGEST NET SALE

No. 2,025. Registered at the G.P.O. as a Newspaper. SATURDAY, APRIL 23, 1910 One Halfpenny.

TO-DAY'S GREAT STRUGGLE FOR THE ENGLISH CUP AT THE CRYSTAL PALACE: PORTRAITS OF THE BARNSLEY AND NEWCASTLE UNITED ELEVENS.

H. NESS. R. DOWNS.

G. UTLEY. MR. J. T. IBBOTSON, THE REFEREE. R. GLENDINNING

F. MEARNS. W. BARTROP. E. GADSBY. G. LILLYCROP. H. TUFNELL. T. FORMAN. T. BOYLE.

To-day's final game in the contest for the English Cup, which is to be played at the Crystal Palace, is of particular interest if only for the reason that all footballers are asking whether Barnsley, a team which has never appeared in the final before, will beat tried and scientific fighters like Newcastle United. The idea that

Barnsley can be beaten is laughed out of court in the Yorkshire town, which has become football mad, and which is sending an army of supporters—both male and female—to cheer their favourites to victory. Above is the Barnsley eleven. The captain is T. Boyle, and the goalkeeper F. Mearns. Every member of the team is an Englishman.

J. HOWIE. A VIEW OF THE CRYSTAL PALACE. A. SHEPHERD.

G. WILSON. W. McCRACKEN. T. WHITSON. J. STEWART.

A. HIGGINS. J. LAWRENCE. W. LOW. P. McWILLIAM. C. VEITCH. J. RUTHERFORD.

Above are portraits of the twelve men from whom the team to represent Newcastle United will be selected. Their captain is C. Veitch, and their goalkeeper J. Lawrence.—(Photographs by *The Daily Mirror*, Taylor, Byker, Sport and General, and C.N.)

ABOVE: The two sides contesting the 1910 FA Cup final featured on the *Daily Mirror's* front page. Referee J. Ibbotson (top centre) is also given prominence.

Palace Hoodoo

Despite having the finest side of the era in the years leading up to the First World War, Newcastle United did not like playing at the Crystal Palace. For some reason they never performed to their high standards at the south London venue; they never won any of their five FA Cup finals there. Some reckoned it was because the grass was too long for their short passing style of play, some considered that United's stars couldn't cope with the razzamatazz of the Cup final, even back then. Many just thought the Crystal Palace had a jinx over the Tyneside club. That was reinforced when, during season 1906/7, as reigning Football League champions, United were drawn against non-league Crystal Palace in the FA Cup first round, and lost 1-0! It was indeed a Crystal Place hoodoo.

FA Cup Finals at the Palace:

1905 v Aston Villa, lost 0-2.
1906 v Everton, lost 0-1.
1908 v Wolverhampton Wanderers, lost 1-3.
1910 v Barnsley, drew 1-1.
1911 v Bradford City, drew 0-0.

CUP FINAL : PHOTOGRAPH SENT BY TELEGRAPH

The toss at Goodison Park yesterday. Veitch, the Newcastle captain, is wearing a striped jersey. The picture was wired from Manchester to London in nine minutes by the Thorne Baker telectrograph.—("Daily Mirror" photograph.)

ABOVE: How the *Daily Mirror* reported United's victory in the replayed 1910 FA Cup final at Goodison Park on Merseyside.

NEWCASTLE AT LAST WIN THE CUP.

Crowd Indignant at Methods Adopted Against Barnsley in Replayed Final.

SHEPHERD SCORES TWICE.

LIVERPOOL, Thursday.—Newcastle United won the English Cup in the replayed final at Everton to-day, beating Barnsley by 2 to 0, but the manner in which they won did not commend itself to the crowd, and before the end cries of "Dirty Newcastle!" were heard on all hands, a state of affairs probably unique in the history of the club.

FA Cup Final 1910

Despite another disappointment at the Crystal Palace arena – United's fifth – the Black 'n' Whites at last lifted their first FA Cup trophy. In a replay on Merseyside Newcastle's celebrated passing style was this time mixed with an aggressive edge to ensure victory. Centre-forward Albert Shepherd ended up the hero of the day, scoring the two goals that brought the trophy to Tyneside. One of his efforts was in fact the first ever penalty kick in a cup final – coolly despatched past Mearns. The England striker wrapped up the game soon afterwards and the FA Cup was presented to skipper Colin Veitch.

Date & venue:	23rd April 1910 at the Crystal Palace. Newcastle United 1(0) Barnsley 1(1).
United:	Lawrence, McCracken, Whitson, Veitch, Low, McWilliam, Rutherford, Howie, Shepherd, Higgins, Wilson.
Barnsley:	Mearns, Downs, Ness, Glendinning, Boyle, Utley, Bartrop, Gadsby, Lillycrop, Tufnell, Forman.
Goals:	United – Rutherford (83m). Barnsley – Tufnell (37m).
Attendance:	76,980.

Date & venue:	28th April 1910 at Goodison Park. Newcastle United 2(0) Barnsley 0(0).
United:	Lawrence, McCracken, Carr, Veitch, Low, McWilliam, Rutherford, Howie, Shepherd, Higgins, Wilson.
Barnsley:	Mearns, Downs, Ness, Glendinning, Boyle, Utley, Bartrop, Gadsby, Lillycrop, Tufnell, Forman.
Goals:	Shepherd (51m, 65m pen).
Attendance:	69,364.
Captain:	Colin Veitch.
Manager:	Director's Committee.

FA Cup Final 1911

United's last final at the old Crystal Palace complex was no better than the first, or the three in between. Once more they failed to deliver at the Sydenham bowl, but they forced a replay once more, this time in Manchester. With a new trophy to play for, made appropriately in Bradford – the existing FA Cup – United missed both Shepherd and McWilliam, two influential players, badly injured just before the final. And that cruel luck proved telling. Bradford capitalized and won the game with a single goal – a soft one at that. United goalkeeper Jimmy Lawrence made a mess of collecting a ball, enabling Speirs to net with ease.

The two captains, United's Colin Veitch (left) and Bradford City's Jimmy Speirs (right) are featured in the *Daily Mirror's* leader for the 1911 FA Cup final.

Date & venue:	22nd April 1911 at the Crystal Palace. Newcastle United 0(0) Bradford City 0(0).
United:	Lawrence, McCracken, Whitson, Veitch, Low, Willis, Rutherford, Stewart, Jobey, Higgins, Wilson.
Bradford City:	Mellors, Campbell, Taylor, Robinson, Gildea, McDonald, Logan, Speirs, O'Rourke, Devine, Thompson.
Goals:	none.
Attendance:	69,800.

Date & venue:	26th April 1911 at Old Trafford. Newcastle United 0(0) Bradford City 1(1).
United:	Lawrence, McCracken, Whitson, Veitch, Low, Willis, Rutherford, Stewart, Jobey, Higgins, Wilson.
Bradford City:	Mellors, Campbell, Taylor, Robinson, Torrance, McDonald, Logan, Speirs, O'Rourke, Devine, Thompson.
Goals:	City – Speirs (15m).
Attendance:	66,646.
Captain:	Colin Veitch.
Manager:	Director's Committee.

W. H. Smith & Son's
SOUVENIR CARD
OF THE
ENGLISH CUP FINAL
1911

COLIN VEITCH

NEWCASTLE UNITED v. BRADFORD CITY
PLAYED AT THE
CRYSTAL PALACE
Saturday, April 22nd
PRICE: ONE PENNY

1911 FA Cup final programme.

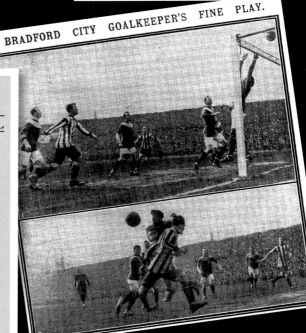

BRADFORD CITY GOALKEEPER'S FINE PLAY.

ABOVE: Action from United's replayed 1911 final at Old Trafford with Bradford's goalkeeper Mark Mellors keeping United at bay.

The First World War

Football continued for a full season during 1914/15 almost without any disruption while fighting on the Continent raged between the Allies and Germany. United finished that programme in 15th position, but long before the end of the season it was clear that the game could not continue as normal. Many players had already started to join Kitchener's call to arms and a halt to football was made at the end of that season. Newcastle United were effectively placed in mothballs until the local Victory League was created in January 1919. Several of Newcastle's players saw battle in Europe, including Donald Bell who won the VC, a reserve amateur at St James' Park in 1912. He was sadly killed in action, one of a handful of United men to perish, including first-team regular Tommy Goodwill.

BELOW: Britain declared hostilities with Germany on 4th August 1914. The *Daily Mirror* reported the news, and the horrific trench warfare that was soon to be found over vast areas of northern Europe. Local regiments, the Northumberland Fusiliers and the Durham Light Infantry sent thousands of men to the front line. Many never returned.

DECLARATION OF WAR BY GREAT BRITAIN AFTER UNSATISFACTORY REPLY TO YESTERDAY'S ULTIMATUM.

LEFT: By the start of 1919 an end was in sight of the dreadful conflict. The *Daily Mirror* made sure news reached Newcastle quickly, by organizing flights to Tyneside, such as the one featured here, on a Vickers aircraft.

The Roaring Twenties & Thirties
1920-1940

High drama at Wembley Stadium in the 1932 FA Cup final: United's equalizing goal against Arsenal made plenty of headlines.

"
Hughie Gallacher is making Newcastle United a bigger power.

All Sports magazine
"

1920 Football gets back to normal, United claiming 8th position in the Division One table. **1921** A 5th place finish maintains United's post-war standing as one of the top clubs. **1922** Jimmy Lawrence completes his final game and establishes a record 496 appearances. **1923** The Magpies finish in 4th place in the First Division ranking. **1924** United visit Wembley for the first time and lift the FA Cup after beating Aston Villa. **1925** Newcastle officials start a transfer chase for the highly rated Scot, Hughie Gallacher. **1926** Record signing Gallacher completes his first season at centre-forward with 25 goals. **1927** Newcastle claim another Football League title victory, with Gallacher's record 36 goals. **1928** United defeat Aston Villa by 7-5 in a remarkable fixture at St James' Park. **1929** A crowd of over 66,000 watch United defeat Sunderland by 4-3 on Tyneside. **1930** Scottish international Andy Cunningham becomes United's first manager. **1931** Gallacher sold to Chelsea and creates a record crowd of 68,386 on his return north. **1932** United defeat Arsenal to lift the FA Cup in the famous "over the line" final. **1933** The Tynesiders compete for the title trophy but end in 5th place. **1934** Newcastle decline dramatically and are relegated into the Second Division. **1935** Andy Cunningham is replaced by Tom Mather in a bid to rebuild the side. **1936** Mediocrity in league action, but an epic FA Cup double meeting with Arsenal. **1937** A promotion bid ends in United finishing in 4th place. **1938** United survive the drop into Division Three for the first time only on goal average. **1939** War halts the 1939/40 season and Stan Seymour starts a rebuilding process.

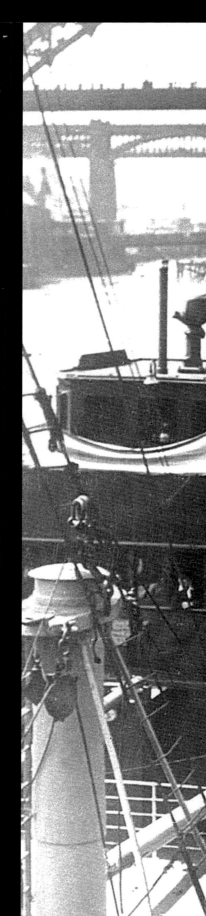

Newcastle Quayside a few days before the 1932 FA Cup final. United's supporters gather for what is now an unusual way of getting to the capital – by Tyne Tees Shipping Co. steamer down the North Sea! The trip cost 25 shillings (£1.25p) for a first-class return ticket.

Like many clubs after the First World War, it took United a couple of years to find their feet following the turmoil of conflict. Newcastle's fine Edwardian side had been broken up and a new team had to be fashioned. The Magpies continued to stand among the elite clubs, and with a new national stadium at Wembley had a new target to focus on. They were one of the first to be triumphant in front of the Twin Towers, and when a new offside rule came into force heralding a flow of goals, became even more of a threat – until a decline in fortune saw relegation from the top tier of football for the very first time.

THE KING TO-DAY OPENS WEMBLEY IN STATE

LEFT: A fine panorama of the Empire Exhibition at Wembley featured on the front page of the *Daily Mirror* in April 1924. At the top of the aerial picture is the new Empire Stadium, to become legendary the world over simply as Wembley. Newcastle took part in that year's FA Cup final and travelling fans could experience the vast exhibition on show.

The SS *Bernicia* leaving Newcastle Quayside packed with the Toon Army of 1924. It was noted that a "great crowd gave them a hearty send-off". It was certainly a different way to get to Wembley.

Ship Shape for Wembley

These days getting to the FA Cup final is an easy task from the North – there are plenty of trains and budget airlines to London, and a rapid motorway system from north to south. In pre-war England though, it was not so easy. Going by road was a gruelling trip and the train was the main form of transport. But some Newcastle supporters even went by sea, down the North Sea coast from the Tyne to the Thames. For both the 1924 and 1932 FA Cup finals excursions were organized from Newcastle Quayside on the steamer Bernicia, with around 300 fans sailing south, all clad in black and white.

FA Cup Final 1924

In only the second final to be staged at the new Empire Stadium in Wembley, and the first all-ticket affair, United were resolute in defence and potent in attack. This was an epic final between two of the country's glamour clubs. For much of the game the contest was evenly played out, but in the final period Newcastle caught Villa with a double strike. The all-important first goal was a superb effort, a three-man move finished off by Neil Harris. Winger Stan Seymour then made it a Tyneside glory day by hitting a fierce drive into the roof of the net.

RIGHT: The *Daily Mirror* preview of the 1924 FA Cup final with United's squad (top) ready for the big day. Fans arrive in London (bottom, left and right).

TO-DAY'S GREAT CUP FINAL AT WEMBLEY: THE RIVAL TEAMS AND THE TROPHY

The Newcastle United team and reserves with their directors at Harrow, where they have been awaiting to-day's final. They are expected to line up as follows: Mutch; Hamp-son and Hudspeth (captain of the team); Mooney, Spencer and Gibson; Low, Cowan, Harris, McDonald and Seymour.

A special train from Newcastle brings supporters to London for to-day's stern struggle. If their team does not win it will not be for lack of encouragement and confidence in the United's ability.

The Cup for which Aston Villa and Newcastle United compete.

George Bellamy, the Newcastle "mascot," who walked all the way from Newcastle, surrounded by fellow-supporters whom he met at King's Cross on their arrival by train yesterday.

The Football Cup Final is due to start in the Wembley Stadium at three o'clock this afternoon, when Aston Villa and Newcastle United meet to decide who shall hold the trophy for the coming year. Pictures of the probable teams appear above, but changes may be made as the health or condition of individual players demands. The result is regarded as fairly open, popular opinion inclining to the belief that Newcastle are stronger in attack, but that the Villa possesses a sound defence.

NEWCASTLE'S GREAT CUP FINAL VICTORY—PICTURE RECORD OF A WELL-FOUGHT GAME

Rival players find the turf treacherous after the morning rain.

Jackson, Aston Villa's goalkeeper, punching out after a corner kick by Newcastle (stripes).

A Villa back robbing a Newcastle forward of the ball.

The Newcastle captain, Hudspeth, being congratulated after receiving the Cup.

The Duke of York and the Villa team.

Date & venue:	26th April 1924 at Wembley Stadium. Newcastle United 2(0) Aston Villa 0(0).
United:	Bradley, Hampson, Hudspeth, Gibson, Spencer, Mooney, Low (J), Cowan, Harris (N), McDonald, Seymour.
Aston Villa:	Jackson, Smart, Mort, Moss, Milne, Blackburn, York, Kirton, Capewell, Walker, Dorrell.
Goals:	Harris (83m), Seymour (86m).
Attendance:	91,695.
Captain:	Frank Hudspeth.
Manager:	Director's Committee.

LEFT: Action at Wembley. Skipper Frank Hudspeth (centre left) takes the FA Cup into the Wembley dressing-room after the 2-0 victory.

FOOTBALL -STATS-

Stan Seymour

Name: George Stanley Seymour

Born: Kelloe 1893

Died: Newcastle upon Tyne 1978

Playing Career: 1909–1929

Clubs: Bradford City, Greenock Morton, Newcastle United

United League & Cup appearances: 266

United League & Cup goals: 84

FA Cup winner 1924, League Champions 1927

England unofficial appearances: 2

> *A magic character. He loved this club and simply lived for football.*
>
> Joe Harvey

1924 FA Cup final programme.

-LEGENDS-

Stan Seymour

They called him... Mr Newcastle

Although born and bred in the North East, Stan Seymour made a name for himself in Scotland before settling on Tyneside, where he became a potent winger, able to link well and score plenty of goals. A regular with the Magpies for nine seasons, he lifted both the FA Cup and Football League title with United before returning as a director – a rarity in football – and guiding the club to their great post-war FA Cup treble. He was known as Mr Newcastle and served the club for almost 50 years.

> *The feeling as we made our way up to Wembley Stadium was one I never forgot.*
>
> Stan Seymour

33

League Champions 1927

Newcastle battled out the title with Huddersfield Town, winners in the past two seasons, and arch local rivals Sunderland. In the end the difference was the goalscoring exploits of Scottish centre-forward Hughie Gallacher, who was an inspiration all season. No defender in the division could handle his brilliance. United's five-man pint-sized forward line – with an average height of 5ft 7ins – was a danger in every match, while veteran Frank Hudspeth marshalled the defence with authority. The winning point was secured in a 1-1 draw at Upton Park against West Ham United.

Record:	P42 W25 D6 L11 F96 A58 – 56 Pts.
Regular side:	Wilson, Maitland, Hudspeth, Gibson, Spencer, McKenzie, Urwin, McKay, Gallacher, McDonald, Seymour.
Top scorers:	Gallacher 36, Seymour 18, McDonald 17.
Captain:	Hughie Gallacher.
Manager:	Director's Committee.

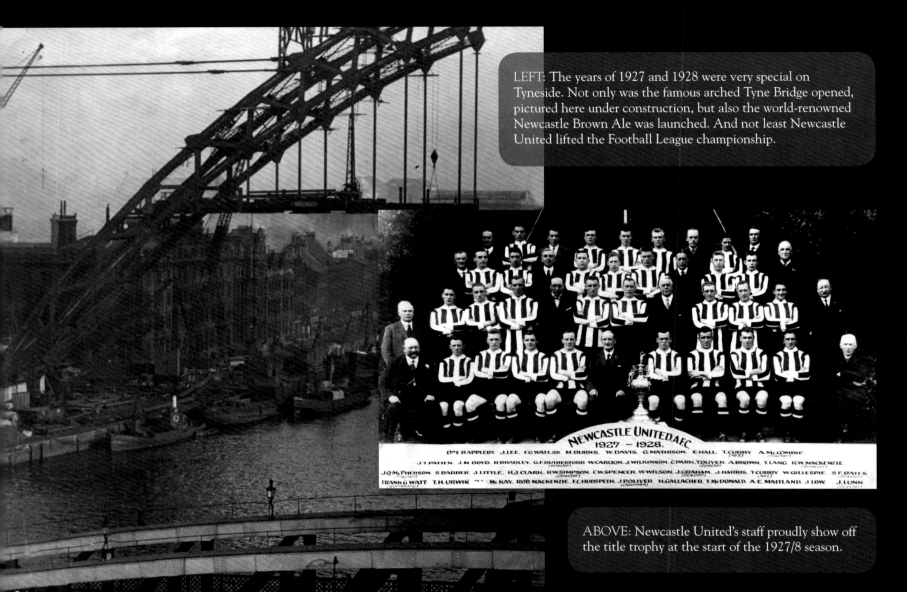

LEFT: The years of 1927 and 1928 were very special on Tyneside. Not only was the famous arched Tyne Bridge opened, pictured here under construction, but also the world-renowned Newcastle Brown Ale was launched. And not least Newcastle United lifted the Football League championship.

ABOVE: Newcastle United's staff proudly show off the title trophy at the start of the 1927/8 season.

–LEGENDS–

Hughie Gallacher

A Wee Scots' genius in attack

A legendary centre-forward who led United to the Football League crown as skipper in 1927. A monumental personality during the inter-war years, Gallacher in many ways was a loveable rascal; a devastating goal-getter even though he was just 5ft 5in tall, he possessed brilliant skills as well as a hot temper that frequently landed him in trouble on the pitch. He was equally in the headlines off the field too, all adding to the colourful character of the Scot. He stood alongside Dixie Dean as Britain's finest, and netted all told over 450 goals in a remarkable career.

ABOVE: One of Gallacher's 36 goals (39 league and cup) in the title winning season – a club record at the time. The Scot heads into the net at St James' Park against Tottenham Hotspur.

FOOTBALL –STATS–

Hughie Gallacher

Name: Hugh Kilpatrick Gallacher

Born: Bellshill 1903

Died: Gateshead 1957

Playing Career: 1919–1939

Clubs: Queen of the South, Airdrieonians, Newcastle United, Chelsea, Derby County, Notts County, Grimsby Town, Gateshead

United League & Cup appearances: 174

United League & Cup goals: 143

League Champions 1927

Scotland appearances: 20

> *He was truly a great centre-forward – and when you consider that Hughie was only 5ft 5in tall, then what he achieved was staggering.*
>
> Tommy Lawton

LEFT: Gallacher became one of football's most talked about figures between the wars, a magnificent footballer.

Record Attendance

3rd September 1930
Newcastle United 1 Chelsea 0

It was perhaps fate that brought supporters' favourite Hughie Gallacher back to Tyneside for the opening home fixture of the new 1930/1 season against Chelsea, this after the Scot had made a controversial and near record move to the Londoners in the summer. Crowds flocked to St James' Park, and estimates reckoned there was over 70,000 trying to gain entry into the Gallowgate arena.

The official attendance was 68,386, a ground record, and one which is unlikely to ever be beaten. Thousands were locked out. All were there to see the return of Gallacher, one of the club's greatest ever players. United won the game by a solitary goal, scored by winger Jackie Cape. Gallacher had his moments but was somewhat overawed by the fantastic reception he received in the blue shirt of Chelsea.

United: McInroy, Nelson, Fairhurst, Mathison, Hill, Naylor, Cape, Starling, Lindsay, McDonald, Wilkinson.
Goals: Cape.

> " I have been sold like a slave for a bag of gold.
>
> Hughie Gallacher "

TOP: Wee Hughie a Chelsea star. Gallacher's move to Stamford Bridge was a highly contentious transfer; both player and fans were against it and when he returned to Gallowgate with his new club, support for the Scot was unprecedented. Note that Hughie in civvies (centre) is smoking, pictured at Stamford Bridge with Andy Wilson and Jackie Crawford, while he is featured (right) with Alec Jackson in training.

RIGHT: Newcastle's victorious party of players and directors ready to head back to Tyneside with the FA Cup. Chairman James Lunn holds the trophy, flanked by Jimmy Nelson (left) and Jimmy Boyd (right).

Goalmouth action from Wembley in 1932: United's Jimmy Richardson is on the ball after an exchange between Allen and Boyd (on the ground).

Wartime to Boomtime
1940-1950

Keeping fit at St James' Park just after the Second World War.
Left to right: Bobby Mitchell, Tommy Walker, Charlie Crowe,
George Robledo and Jack Milburn.

> " *Newcastle United faced the future with tremendous resources and with great confidence.* "
>
> Jack Milburn

1940 United reach the War Cup semi-final, but lose to Blackburn Rovers. **1941** The Black 'n' Whites again fall at the semi-final stage, this time to Preston. **1942** United play derby fixtures with Gateshead on a regular basis. **1943** The Magpies net goals galore, including a 9-0 victory over Leeds. **1944** Goalscoring machine Albert Stubbins grabs 43 goals in the season. **1945** Peace is restored and football starts to get back to normality. **1946** Newcastle rack up a 13-0 victory over Newport County, a record scoreline. **1947** Crowds boom as United become big spenders in a bid to get back into the elite. **1948** United win promotion in front of an average home gate of over 56,000. **1949** United lose the title to Portsmouth, but are back with the best in football. **1950** Another championship race with Pompey, but United finish three points adrift.

The Second World War

United's last match before the Second World War broke out was a resounding 8-1 victory over Swansea Town in September 1939. Soon afterwards the new 1939/40 season was scrapped and "wartime football" arrived. Unlike the First World War, United took part in the hastily formed regional leagues from the start and produced a free-scoring line-up which included many guests, players such as Tom Finney, Stan Mortensen and Bill Nicholson. They also fielded the country's top goal-getter in Albert Stubbins who netted over 230 goals during those years of conflict. As a result high-scoring came frequently, the Magpies thrashing Leeds United 9-0, Bradford City and Middlesbrough by all of 11-0, while there was an amazing 6-6 draw with Gateshead!

A wintery Gallowgate scene as Newcastle face Charlton Athletic with goalkeeper Sam Bartram about to challenge Jackie Milburn for the ball.

In many ways the Second World War came at the right time for Newcastle United. They needed a period to repair a broken club and with ex-star player Stan Seymour at the helm, the five war years were used to overhaul the St James' Park set-up from top to bottom. Many young stars in the making pulled on the black and white shirt at that time and in the boom seasons as peace was restored, United also became one of football's big spenders, bringing plenty of expensive stars to Gallowgate. That blend of home-grown talent and big-money buys worked a treat.

VE-DA

RIGHT: Germany surrendered on 7th May 1945 and VE-Day – Victory in Europe day – took place on the following day, 8th May. The *Daily Mirror*, like every other newspaper, celebrated the occasion. With peace restored football was to get quickly back to normal.

LEFT: War raged for over five years, and everyone an was affected. Pictured here are two wardens fully kitt streets of Newcastle in 1939.

Veterans and Youngsters

Heading to Anfield

ABOVE: Wartime goalscoring machine Albert Stubbins wanted top-flight football and headed for Liverpool in a near record deal of £12,500 during September 1946. He netted an amazing 237 goals for United and went on to lift the title and FA Cup at Anfield.

ABOVE LEFT: Newcastle's immediate post-war line-up was an effective blend of veteran pre-war players and bright youngsters eager to impress. Benny Craig was one of the experienced men from Thirties football. He remained at Gallowgate as coach and physio until the 1980s.

ABOVE RIGHT: A young Ashington forward called Jack Milburn earned a trial with United in 1943. He impressed all and began the post-war era running the wing. He was soon to take the centre-forward's role and cause quite an impact.

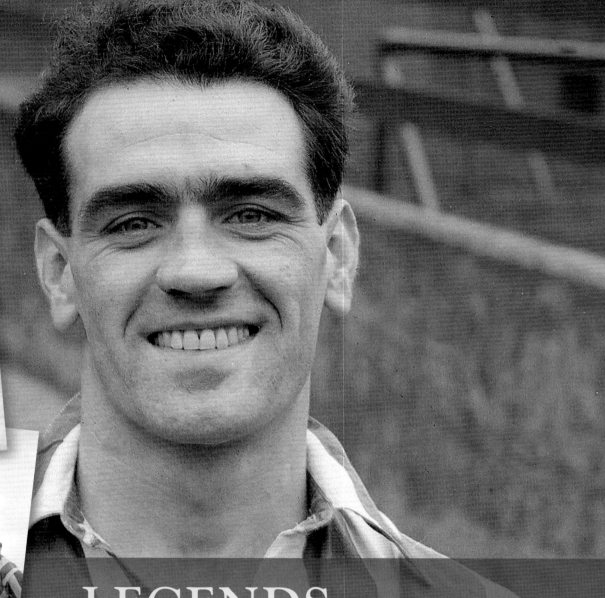

FOOTBALL
—STATS—

Joe Harvey

Name: Joseph Harvey

Born: Edlington 1918

Died: Newcastle upon Tyne 1989

Playing Career: 1936–1954

Clubs: Wolves, Bournemouth, Bradford City, Newcastle United

United League & Cup appearances: 247

United League & Cup goals: 12

FA Cup winner 1951, 1952

Football League appearances: 3

—LEGENDS—

Joe Harvey

The Yorkshire Geordie, black and white at heart

Player, skipper, coach, manager and scout of Newcastle United in a career with the club spanning more than 35 years. Joe Harvey led United back into the top flight after the war, then twice lifted the FA Cup at Wembley as a gritty right-half who inspired all. He was then coach to another victory and soon returned as manager in 1962 to rebuild the club, guiding the Magpies to first promotion, then to a European victory and back to Wembley in yet another FA Cup final.

> *Joe was a gem –
> a man's man.*
>
> Malcolm Macdonald

Joe Harvey was a fine footballer with a resolute and courageous attitude. In midfield or defence he always gave his all.

49

Big Spenders

In spite of United's Second Division status at the start of the immediate post-war years, the Magpies became the country's big spenders as football returned to normal. Newcastle searched for talent in England and Scotland and brought a host of quality footballers to Tyneside. They continually paid big transfer fees in the years up to 1950 to build their next great side.

- Len Shackleton £13,000 from Bradford Park Avenue.
- Colin Gibson £15,000 from Cardiff City.
- Frank Brennan £7,500 from Airdrie.
- George & Ted Robledo £23,000 from Barnsley.
- Bobby Mitchell £17,000 from Third Lanark.
- Roy Bentley £8,500 from Bristol City.
- George Lowrie £18,500 from Coventry City.

Home-grown Talent

At the same time as spending big in the transfer market, United developed their own talent, many stars of the future arriving at St James' Park from the proverbial pit-heads of Northumberland or County Durham. Included were Jackie Milburn, Bobby Cowell, Charlie Wayman, Ernie Taylor, Charlie Crowe and Bob Stokoe.

Big Scot Frank Brennan was one of the new arrivals on Tyneside. A Scottish international centre-half, he quickly became a crowd favourite and the cornerstone to United's defence. Few strikers got the better of the 6ft 3in stopper.

Record Victory

5th October 1946

Newcastle United 13 Newport County 0

When a resurgent Magpies faced an aging Newport County side early into the 1946/7 season few could have guessed what the outcome would have been. With a side packed with both youthful talent like Jackie Milburn as well as big-transfer purchases such as Len Shackleton – who was making his debut – Newcastle totally dominated proceedings and raced to a record 13-0 victory. In front of a crowd of over 52,000, the rout began when Wayman headed home, a chance made by Shackleton. United's new inside-forward was soon on the scoresheet and he went on to score no fewer than six goals. Shack's double hat-trick on his first United appearance was sensational. The scoreline remains the highest ever recorded in the top two divisions of English Football. And it could have been more as United also missed a penalty after only 90 seconds!

United: Garbutt, Cowell, Graham, Harvey, Brennan, Wright, Milburn, Bentley, Wayman, Shackleton, Pearson.

Goals: Shackleton (6), Wayman (4), Milburn (2), Bentley.

Newcastle United v Newport programme.

> " *And they were lucky to get none.*
>
> Len Shackleton "

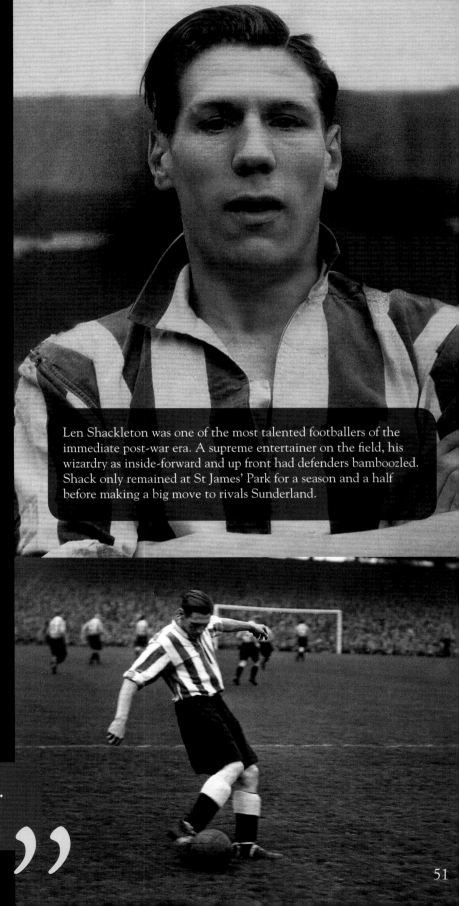

Len Shackleton was one of the most talented footballers of the immediate post-war era. A supreme entertainer on the field, his wizardry as inside-forward and up front had defenders bamboozled. Shack only remained at St James' Park for a season and a half before making a big move to rivals Sunderland.

Sign Please, Mister!

LEFT: Between the posts Jack Fairbrother claimed the No. 1 spot. Signed from Preston North End, he was an experienced goalkeeper, pictured here against Huddersfield Town.

Another of United's wartime finds was diminutive Ernie Taylor, a 5ft 4in tall gem in midfield. The locally born schemer linked perfectly with Jack Milburn in attack.

Another acrobatic stop, this time in training at Gallowgate by Fairbrother's rival as custodian, Eric Garbutt.

Young Jackie... on his way to the Top

The pick of United's youngsters was Jackie Milburn, in action scoring against Wolves in 1948. He quickly caught the eye and was to be the Magpies' top scorer as they claimed a promotion spot. He was soon elevated to the international scene as well.

Promotion 1948

It did not take long for a revamped Magpie side to claim their place back in the top tier of English football. With that fine blend of home-grown talent and big money buys, the Magpies fielded a side packed with star quality, and many were to become internationals over the coming years. The Black 'n' Whites were in contention for most of the season and by Easter were firm favourites for promotion. Over 66,000 witnessed the deciding clash with rivals Sheffield Wednesday at St James' Park, in which United clinched the two points required after a thrilling end-to-end 4-2 victory.

Record: P42 W24 D8 L10 F72 A41 – 56 Pts – Position 2nd.

Regular side: Fairbrother, Cowell or Fraser, Craig, Harvey, Brennan, Dodgin, Sibley, Stobbart, Milburn, Shackleton, Pearson.

Top scorers: Milburn 20, Stobbart 9.

Captain: Joe Harvey.

Manager: George Martin.

BACKGROUND: Another big signing was Chilean striker George Robledo, who arrived at Gallowgate along with his brother Ted as Newcastle began to challenge for the First Division title. George became a feared striker and immensely popular on Tyneside, scoring almost 100 goals before returning to South America in 1953. Another talented import – this time from nearer to home, in Northern Ireland – full-back Alf McMichael is in the background getting a top-up.

LEFT: Also to arrive from Ulster was George Hannah, an influential schemer who remained with Newcastle for eight years.

Off to Brazil

Jack Milburn is pictured near the top of the steps with his England colleagues as they board a plane bound for Rio in 1950.

LEFT: Jackie Milburn was first capped by England in 1950 and was selected for the World Cup squad to travel to Brazil in that year. He faced team-mate George Robledo on that stage, with Chile matched against England in the first group matches.

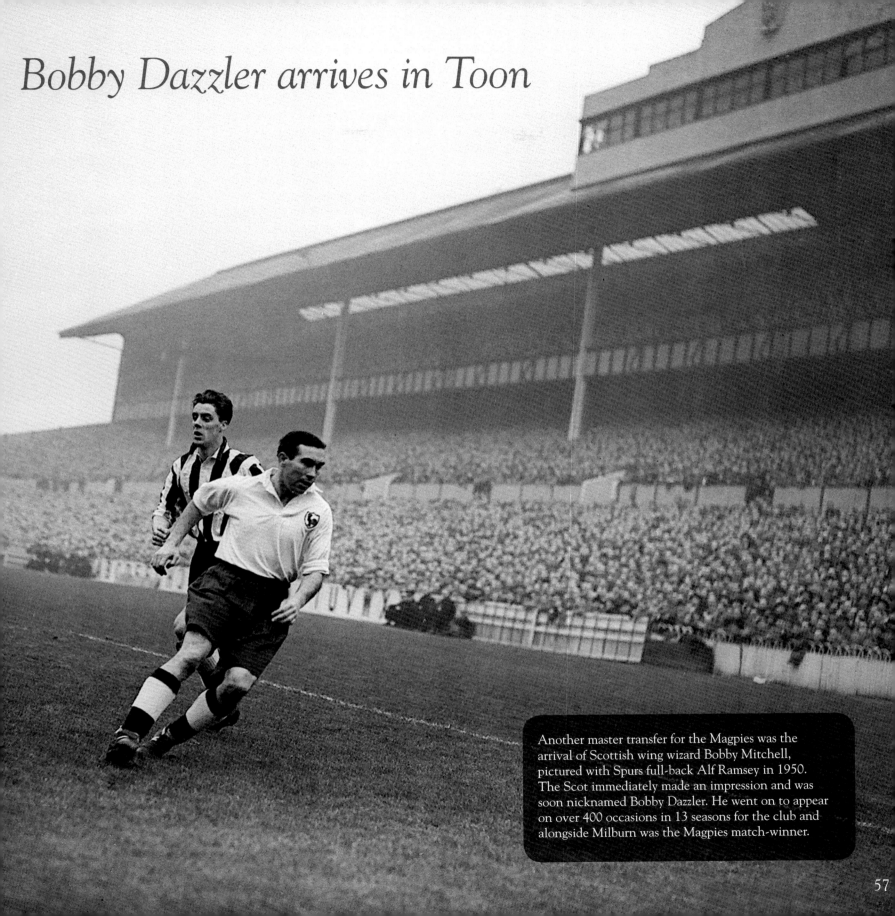

Bobby Dazzler arrives in Toon

Another master transfer for the Magpies was the arrival of Scottish wing wizard Bobby Mitchell, pictured with Spurs full-back Alf Ramsey in 1950. The Scot immediately made an impression and was soon nicknamed Bobby Dazzler. He went on to appear on over 400 occasions in 13 seasons for the club and alongside Milburn was the Magpies match-winner.

Wembley Glory
1950-1961

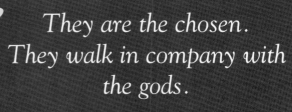

> "They are the chosen. They walk in company with the gods."
>
> Bob Ferrier

United reached three FA Cup finals in five years and lifted the trophy on each occasion to become one of the country's favourite sides. Pictured here is Jack Milburn striking the ball past Blackpool's George Farm in 1951 – the start of United's 1950s glory days.

1951 Two goals from Jackie Milburn win the FA Cup against Blackpool. **1952** Another FA Cup victory at Wembley, this time against Arsenal. **1953** United enter the floodlit age at Gallowgate with a fixture against Celtic. **1954** A crowd of 65,334 sees the opening fixture of the season between United and Arsenal. **1955** United's third FA Cup victory in five years as they overwhelm Manchester City. **1956** Newcastle defeat Sunderland 6-1 and 3-1 in the space of two days during the season. **1957** United win a thrilling FA Cup tie with Manchester City by 5-4. **1958** Charlie Mitten takes over as boss of United and starts to modernize the club. **1959** A trio of stars in Len White, George Eastham and Ivor Allchurch entertain all. **1960** United defeat Manchester United 7-3 in front of over 57,000. **1961** Newcastle tumble into the Second Division again and need a root and branch reform.

Tyneside welcomed back their victorious FA Cup heroes on three occasions. The streets of Newcastle were packed solid with a mass of cheering Geordies as the trophy was paraded through the city, here nearing Grey's Monument.

Mawson Swan & Morgan Ltd

By the time the 1950s had opened, United's new look side was well established, challenging at the top of the table and soon to become an all-conquering combination in the FA Cup. The Black 'n' Whites became the first team since Blackburn Rovers' Victorian eleven to lift the trophy in successive years – and they also claimed the famous "pot" for a third time, all within five seasons. With stars such as Jackie Milburn, Bobby Mitchell, George Robledo and Frank Brennan at the heart of the side, the Tynesiders were one of the most prominent in the country.

En Route for a Wembley Treble

ABOVE: In the 1950/1 FA Cup run to Wembley, United met Bristol Rovers in a two-game epic which had all the ingredients of a David v Goliath clash. The Black 'n' Whites went through after a replay at Eastville: pictured here is Charlie Crowe (far left) finding the net as United won 3-1.

A tough contest followed against Wolverhampton Wanderers in the semi-final, a club of equal standing to the Magpies in the top tier of football. Again the match needed a replay – at Leeds Road, Huddersfield – to settle the issue. United won 2-1: George Robledo is featured getting in a header despite the attention of Billy Wright.

FA Cup Final 1951

Although most of the country wanted to see Blackpool's Stanley Matthews create all the headlines and win a FA Cup winner's medal, it was United's golden boy Jackie Milburn who stole the show with a brace of winning goals inside five minutes. Firing home two wonderful second-half gems – the first a solo 40-yard break-away, the second a 30-yard thunderbolt after a great move from defence and cheeky back-heel pass – Wor Jackie was the talk of the capital. Milburn was rapidly elevated onto the national stage, one of the country's most popular footballers.

Date & venue:	28th April 1951 at Wembley Stadium. Newcastle United 2(0) Blackpool 0(0).
United:	Fairbrother, Cowell, Corbett, Harvey, Brennan, Crowe, Walker, Taylor, Milburn, Robledo (G), Mitchell.
Blackpool:	Farm, Shimwell, Garrett, Johnston, Hayward, Kelly, Matthews, Mudie, Mortensen, Slater, Perry.
Goals:	Milburn (50m, 55m).
Attendance:	100,000.
Captain:	Joe Harvey.
Manager:	Director's Committee/Stan Seymour.

> " It was definitely Milburn's match! His terrific speed made the first. The second was right out of this world! It was the greatest goal I have ever seen.
>
> Stanley Matthews "

Another view of Jackie Milburn's opening goal against Blackpool. His double-strike on that afternoon has gone down in FA Cup history as one of the best ever performances in a Wembley showpiece.

FA Cup Final 1952

United successfully defended their trophy and became the first club for 60 years to lift the FA Cup in successive seasons. Arsenal, however, were handicapped in those pre-substitute days by losing full-back Wally Barnes on 18 minutes, when he was injured tackling Milburn. Newcastle were given the advantage and made it pay, despite the Londoners' battling display. But Newcastle left it late, grabbing a winner in the 84th minute. A typical mesmerizing run by Bobby Mitchell resulted in a cross to the far post and Chilean striker George Robledo headed into the net off the woodwork.

Date & venue:	3rd May 1952 at Wembley Stadium. Newcastle United 1(0) Arsenal 0(0).
United:	Simpson, Cowell, McMichael, Harvey, Brennan, Robledo (E), Walker, Foulkes, Milburn, Robledo (G), Mitchell.
Arsenal:	Swindin, Barnes, Smith, Forbes, Daniel, Mercer, Cox, Logie, Holton, Lishman, Roper.
Goals:	Robledo (G) (84m).
Attendance:	100,000.
Captain:	Joe Harvey.
Manager:	Director's Committee/Stan Seymour.

> " *I nearly passed out as the ball hit the post and went into the net.* "
>
> George Robledo

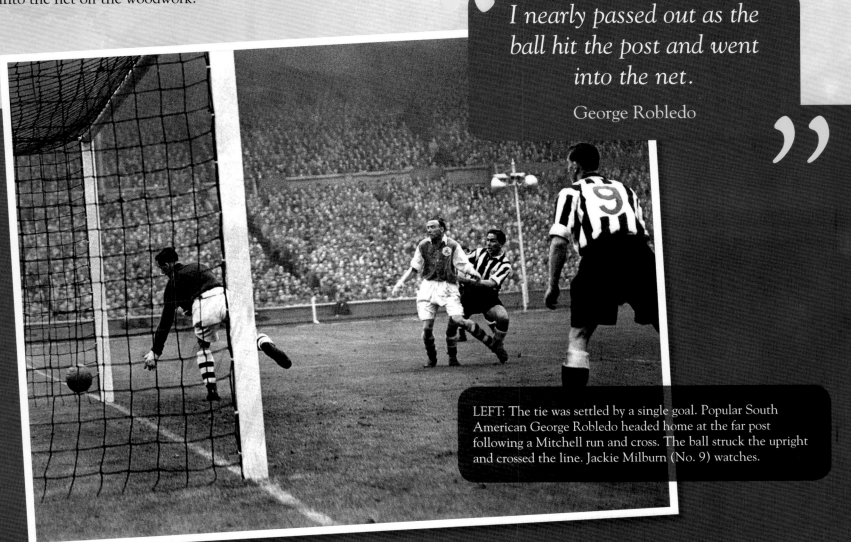

LEFT: The tie was settled by a single goal. Popular South American George Robledo headed home at the far post following a Mitchell run and cross. The ball struck the upright and crossed the line. Jackie Milburn (No. 9) watches.

Joe Harvey re-united with the FA Cup is hoisted on the shoulders of Frank Brennan (left) and George Robledo (right). Also in the picture are, left to right: Ronnie Simpson, Bill Foulkes, Bobby Mitchell and Bobby Cowell.

Dressing-room celebrations beneath the Wembley terracing. Back row, left to right: Ted Robledo, Stan Seymour, Joe Harvey, Frank Brennan, George Robledo (behind), trainer Norman Smith, Bobby Mitchell, Ronnie Simpson. Sitting: Bobby Cowell, Tommy Walker, Bill Foulkes, Alf McMichael and Jack Milburn.

All quiet before...

Newcastle Central Station gets ready for the arrival back on Tyneside of United's "Cup Train". Banners and flags are out. Not a supporter is in sight. That would soon change.

WELCOME HYEM CANNY LADS

LEFT & RIGHT: Over 250,000 fans filled the streets of Newcastle as the train crossed the Tyne Bridge from Kings Cross. A procession of open-topped coaches flanked by police outriders snaked its way through the city with supporters at every vantage point, some on highly precarious ledges and rooftops.

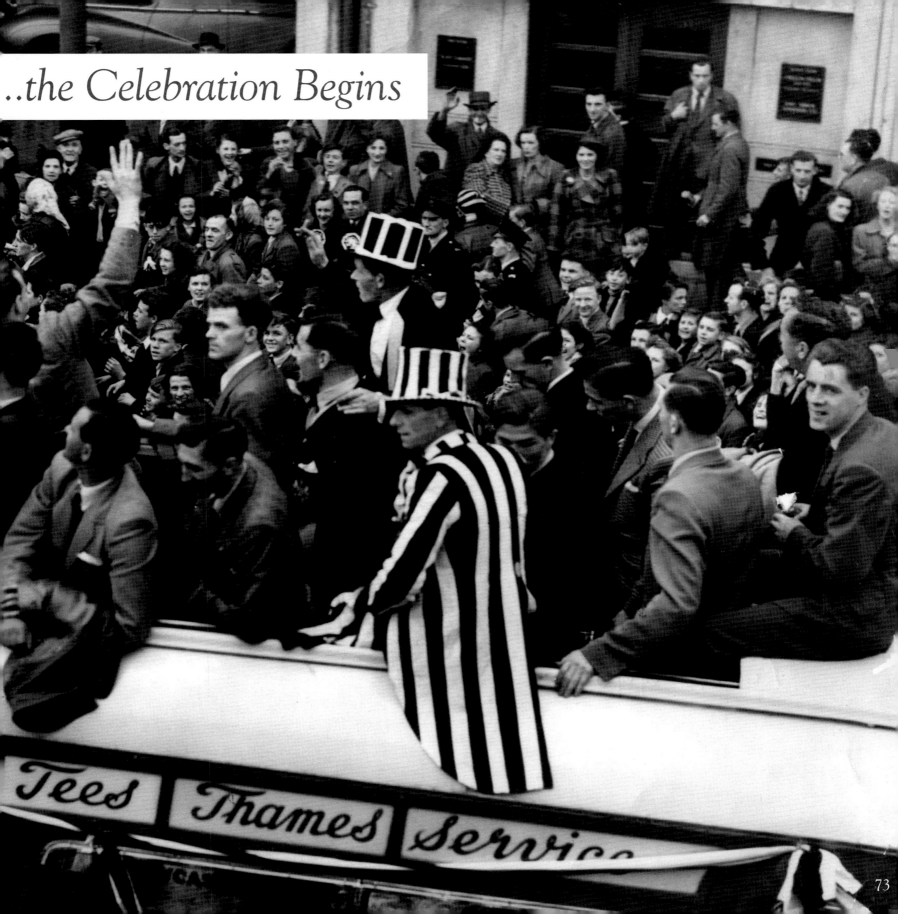

..the Celebration Begins

–LEGENDS–

Jackie Milburn

Gentleman Jackie, on and off the field

Known throughout the football world as Wor Jackie, a legendary centre-forward of the immediate post-war years. With devastating pace and awesome shooting, Milburn was one of the best strikers around while his FA Cup exploits with United – notably a double strike at Wembley in 1951 – made him a Geordie icon, a status which has carried on long past his final day. Born into the famous Milburn and Charlton Ashington football dynasty, Jackie was made a Freeman of Newcastle.

RIGHT: At one stage during the Fifties, Milburn ran a coach tour business serving Northumberland. And he even washed the bus too!

FOOTBALL –STATS–

Jackie Milburn

Name: John Edward Thompson Milburn

Born: Ashington 1924

Died: Ashington 1988

Playing Career: 1943–1960

Clubs: Newcastle United, Linfield

United League & Cup appearances: 397

United League & Cup goals: 200

FA Cup winner 1951, 1952, 1955

England appearances: 13

LEFT: Milburn's pace and shooting power were renowned. In full flow he was a thrill to watch.

The local hero in quiet contemplation. Jackie was never one for headlines or publicity. He was a down-to-earth Ashington lad with a great talent for football.

> "He was the fastest thing in football, and won worldwide admiration."
>
> Sir Tom Finney

RIGHT: By the time United embarked on their third successful FA Cup run, Vic Keeble had taken over the centre-forward role, with Milburn now in support. Something of an aerial artiste, Keeble was a very different kind of striker, yet still effective. He is captured by the camera at St James' Park against Derby County.

George Robledo provided a perfect contrast to Milburn's style; he was robust and a deadly finisher. Defenders did not like his aggressive play, seen here netting in a marvellous 3-0 FA Cup victory over Spurs in 1952. A crowd of 69,009 watched the Magpies' terrific show at White Hart Lane.

The Toon Army of the Fifties

Throughout the Forties and Fifties, United's support was as phenomenal as it is now. Newcastle paraded an official supporter mascot as a cheer-leader in those days. Decked out in black and white of course, he is pictured orchestrating songs at the Leazes End of the Gallowgate stadium.

Newcastle fans in the capital's Trafalgar Square before the 1955 FA Cup final. Fashion and hair styles may have been different, but a Geordie outing to the final was just the same in the Fifties as in the Nineties.

WAGS – Fifties Style

These days we have Posh Spice and Cheryl Cole, as well as Coleen Rooney. Footballers WAGS create as many headlines as the players themselves. It was never quite like that *When Football Was Football* in the Golden Age of the game. Some of Newcastle United's Fifties stars' WAGs are captured by the camera, but none ever made the front or inside pages of the tabloids!

ABOVE: A family shot of Bobby Mitchell and wife, with their two children.

BACKGROUND A group of player WAGs dressed to kill and about to board the train to King's Cross for the 1955 FA Cup final.

LEFT: The better-half of Newcastle United having afternoon tea at their London hotel before the 1952 FA Cup final.

BACKGROUND: Jimmy Scoular shows off the FA Cup to his wife following United's victory at Wembley in 1955.

On our way to Wembley – Yet Again

LEFT: Newcastle faced a testing time in the 1955 FA Cup run with replays against Nottingham Forest then Huddersfield Town in the quarter-final. Pictured is Vic Keeble, in a plain white change shirt, against the Tykes at St James' Park. United won 2-0.

ABOVE: Also to emerge in United's ranks by 1955 was Len White, who claimed a position on the wing. He is seen in the thick of the action in the same tie against Huddersfield with Keeble alongside. White was soon to switch role and take the No. 9 shirt, becoming an instant hit.

ABOVE: Former Portsmouth star Jimmy Scoular took over from Joe Harvey as both United skipper and the team's driving force for the 1955 FA Cup victory. The Scottish international leads the Black 'n' Whites out at Wembley against Manchester City. Behind Scoular are Bobby Cowell, Ron Batty, Jack Milburn and Bobby Mitchell (with the ball).

RIGHT: 1955 FA Cup final programme.

FAR RIGHT: Newcastle's third goal, which all but claimed the trophy for the Tynesiders. Mitchell (No. 11) dribbled to the touchline, pulled the ball back and George Hannah (third from the right) slid the ball past City's German goalkeeper, Bert Trautmann.

THE FOOTBALL ASSOCIATION CHALLENGE CUP COMPETITION

FINAL TIE

MANCHESTER CITY
V
NEWCASTLE UNITED

SATURDAY, MAY 7th, 1955   KICK-OFF 3 pm

EMPIRE STADIUM

WEMBLEY

Chairman and Managing Director   SIR ARTHUR J. ELVIN, MBE
OFFICIAL PROGRAMME · **ONE SHILLING**

FA Cup Final 1955

For the third time in five years the Magpies lifted the FA Cup after a convincing victory over Manchester City. Again Newcastle were fortunate, since City, like Arsenal before them, were forced to play with 10 men when Jimmy Meadows went off injured after trying to stop the wizardry of Mitchell on 30 minutes. Jackie Milburn again created headlines, scoring what was then the fastest ever goal at Wembley – a marvellous header after only 45 seconds. City hit back though, but Newcastle cruised home in the second period making the extra man pay dividends.

Date & venue:	7th May 1955 at Wembley Stadium. Newcastle United 3(1) Manchester City 1(1).
United:	Simpson, Cowell, Batty, Scoular, Stokoe, Casey, White, Milburn, Keeble, Hannah, Mitchell.
Manchester City:	Trautmann, Meadows, Little, Barnes, Ewing, Paul, Spurdle, Hayes, Revie, Johnstone, Fagan.
Goals:	United – Milburn (1m), Mitchell (53m), Hannah (58m). City – Johnstone (44m).
Attendance:	100,000.
Captain:	Jimmy Scoular.
Manager:	Duggie Livingstone.

> " *The better team won.*
>
> Don Revie "

85

LEFT: The Wembley dressing-room was a familiar location for the Black 'n' Whites. Left to right: Stan Seymour (director), Bobby Cowell, Vic Keeble, Ron Batty, Tommy Casey (with trophy), Duggie Livingstone (manager) and Norman Smith (trainer).

BELOW: Left to right: Norman Smith (trainer), George Hannah, Alex Mutch (physio), Bobby Mitchell, Jack Milburn, Tommy Casey, Bob Stokoe.

In the Boardroom

For over a 100 years Newcastle United were controlled at the top by generation after generation of directors either linked by family or friendship way back to when the club first became a limited company in 1890. Over that period, ownership and control of the Magpies was restricted to holders of the 2,000 ten-shilling shares, with ultimate control of the transfer or sale of such shares. It was in many respects a closed-shop until Sir John Hall's takeover, when, ironically, the new ownership of Newcastle United was held by virtually one family. Past names with a major say in how the Black 'n' Whites were run include the Bells, Olivers, Rutherfords and McKeags, as well as Lord Westwood and his father.

FAR LEFT: While Newcastle employed a manager for that 1955 triumph, Duggie Livingstone, power in the player camp largely rested with former 1920s favourite Stan Seymour. He was influential in all the club's immediate post-war success, promotion and a treble of FA Cup wins.

LEFT: The most noted of Seymour's colleagues – and often rivals – at board level was Alderman William McKeag (right), a monocled solicitor and former MP, pictured with later club Secretary Dennis Barker. His son, Gordon McKeag, was a rival with John Hall for control of the club at the end of the Nineties.

BELOW: Apart from the powerful Seymour, United's Board of Directors consisted of several other high-profile characters. Indeed, the politics behind the scenes at St James' Park was as eventful as the football on the pitch. Left to right: Robert Rutherford, William McKeag, John Lee and Secretary Ted Hall.

Following the break-up of United's fine post-war FA Cup side, United boldly moved into what was a changing football scene by appointing a young, bright and progressive-thinking manager in Charlie Mitten during the summer of 1958. The former Manchester United player was something of a controversial character, but he did try to modernize the club and did bring together an exquisite trio of Len White, George Eastham and Ivor Allchurch in Magpie colours. Yet Mitten's fresh approach brought with it relegation in 1961, and so it was back to the drawing-board for the Gallowgate club.

RIGHT: Charlie Mitten had new ideas – and a love of greyhounds which ended up in Newcastle United's treatment-room as often as the players! Director Wally Hurford is pictured with Mitten.

Newcastle players relax with a game of snooker. Bob Stokoe concentrates with the cue, watched by, right to left, Bill Punton, Bill Curry, Dick Keith, Bobby Mitchell and Len White.

A Majestic Trio

Many judges reckoned Ivor Allchurch was the very best of several great Welsh players of the era, the Golden Boy of Wales. He joined United in a headline deal in 1958. A midfielder who could dominate the play, he was to gel with the up-and-coming George Eastham and goal-power of Len White almost to perfection. Ivor is pictured against Manchester United at Old Trafford.

RIGHT: Small and stocky, the former miner Len White is caught by the camera jumping with Portsmouth's Jimmy Dickinson. He was to net 108 goals for the Magpies in only four seasons. Such was his popularity that many supporters of the day rated him on equal standing with Jackie Milburn.

BELOW: George Eastham hailed from a noted footballing family – as did both White and Allchurch – and was the youngest of the trio. He quickly blossomed into a midfield talent destined for the top. Yet this magical threesome could not stop United's decline and relegation. By the time that happened, Eastham had fallen into major dispute not only with United but also football's authorities over an antiquated transfer system – all to end up in the High Court and victory for the player.

Floodlit Football Arrives

Although United's first taste of floodlit football on Tyneside was back in 1953 when the Magpies faced Glasgow Celtic under the lights, Football League contests did not arrive until the 1955/6 season.

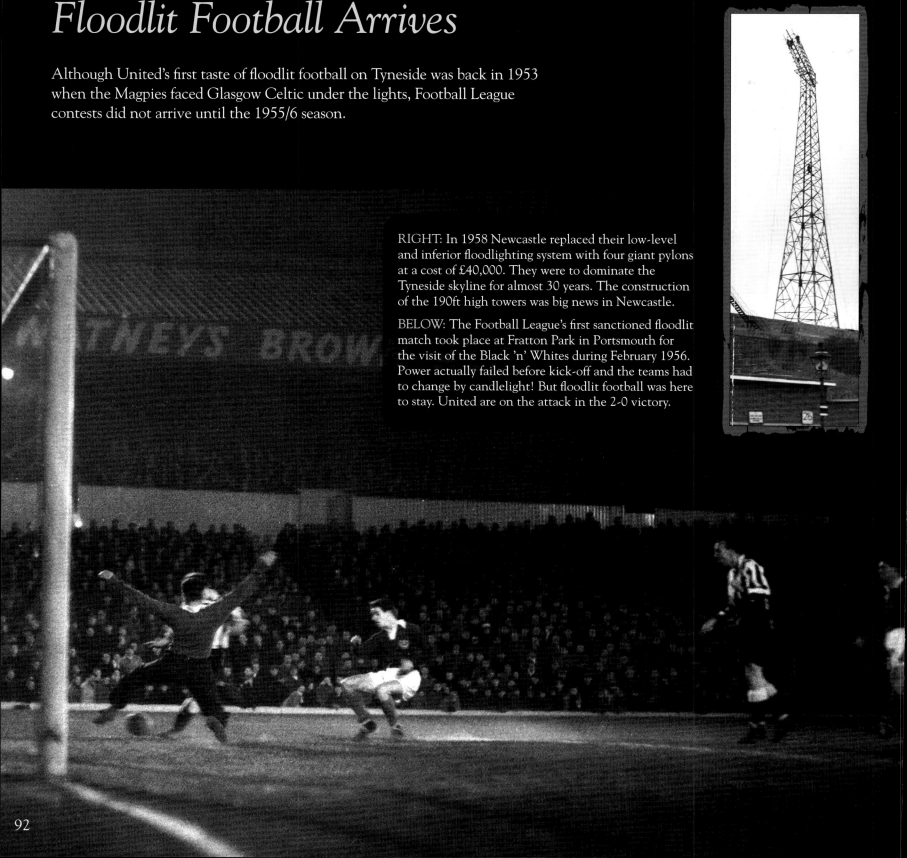

RIGHT: In 1958 Newcastle replaced their low-level and inferior floodlighting system with four giant pylons at a cost of £40,000. They were to dominate the Tyneside skyline for almost 30 years. The construction of the 190ft high towers was big news in Newcastle.

BELOW: The Football League's first sanctioned floodlit match took place at Fratton Park in Portsmouth for the visit of the Black 'n' Whites during February 1956. Power actually failed before kick-off and the teams had to change by candlelight! But floodlit football was here to stay. United are on the attack in the 2-0 victory.

St James' Park

A Fortress for over a century.

One of the oldest football stadiums in the country and situated in the very heart of the city, St James' Park was first used in 1880 when pathfinder club Newcastle Rangers kicked a ball around on what was then only a rough patch of grass, part of the vast Town Moor parkland. Newcastle West End had a home there, then Newcastle United's pioneers, East End, moved to the site in 1892; and afterwards the arena started to take shape.

Development took place for United's entry into the top tier of football in 1898, then a major revamp was undertaken in 1905. But for well over 80 years afterwards, the story of the development of the Magpies' home was one of controversy. Not until Sir John Hall's takeover at the start of the 1990s was St James' Park transformed into a modern stadium. By 1994 a 36,000 all-seater arena was completed, being enlarged for the 2000/1 season to the present capacity of over 52,000.

Present capacity: 52,387.

Record attendance: 68,386 v Chelsea, September 1930.

Record average attendance: 56,299, 1947/8 season, Division Two.

RIGHT: Apart from the addition of floodlight towers, St James' Park had remained largely unaltered since the ground was redeveloped back in 1905. The main West Stand, with its bird's-eye press-box, remained a feature of the stadium as pictured (right) on this winter's scene. Much needed modernization was soon to become a bitter political football dispute between club and landlord, the City Council.

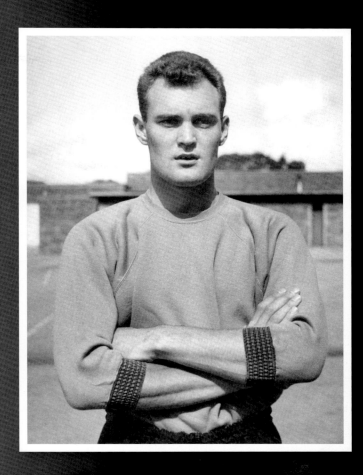

BACKGROUND: Action at Old Trafford in 1959. Manchester United's Bobby Charlton – from the Ashington Milburn stock – leaps with Newcastle goalkeeper Bryan Harvey. Jimmy Scoular looks on.

RIGHT: Bryan Harvey was kept a busy goalkeeper as Newcastle battled against the drop in the 1960/1 season. His defence was a problem throughout that season, with United conceding 109 goals.

ABOVE: Charlie Mitten's squad struggled against relegation and looked doomed. Players in training at St James' Park are, left to right: George Dalton, Dick Keith and Ivor Allchurch. They are marshalled by trainers at the end of the rope, Benny Craig (left) and Norman Smith (right).

BACKGROUND: Newcastle relied much on Len White in a bid to retain their senior status in 1960/1. United's centre-forward goes for goal against Manchester United and is stopped by a Harry Gregg save. A reckless tackle by Tottenham's Dave MacKay at White Hart Lane put him on the sidelines at a crucial time in the relegation fight.

Fighting the Drop

On paper Newcastle United had what looked like a decent side, with experienced heads like Jimmy Scoular, here in action chasing Chelsea's new star Jimmy Greaves at Stamford Bridge. They also fielded the ability of Alf McMichael, Bob Stokoe and Bobby Mitchell – as well as the Allchurch, White and Eastham trio. Nevertheless, United's Fifties' glory days were over.

European Adventure
1961-1975

Following a successful remodelling of the squad at St James' Park, the Magpies experienced their first taste of European action in the now quickly developing football world. Remarkably, United won a trophy at the first attempt and the Gallowgate stadium was filled to capacity as crack Hungarians Újpesti Dózsa were toppled in 1969. Bob Moncur leaps in the air as Newcastle score, while Bryan Robson watches. Note the supporters on the roof tops of Leazes Terrace.

> "We were a team in the best sense of the word. There were no superstars, no world-beaters, just a damned good team.
>
> Jim Scott

1962 Ex-skipper Joe Harvey returns as boss
and begins a new era at St James' Park.
1963 Snow disrupts football as the FA Cup
match with Bradford City is postponed 12
times. 1964 Headlines made as United are
knocked out of the FA Cup by minnows
Bedford Town. 1965 Newcastle are Second
Division champions and return to the First
Division. 1966 A search for big stars begins
as Wyn Davies makes a record move to
St James' Park. 1967 United just survive
the drop as the Magpies struggle to score
goals. 1968 Newcastle qualify for European
football for the first time. 1969 United enter
Europe and shock everyone by winning the
Inter Cities Fairs Cup. 1970 Defending
the trophy, United reach the quarter-finals
before a cruel exit. 1971 More Euro action
as the Magpies see off Inter Milan in an
exhilarating tie. 1972 With new signing
Malcolm Macdonald in the No. 9 shirt,
United make headlines. 1973 Flamboyant
stars catch the eye: Jimmy Smith, Tony
Green and Terry Hibbitt included. 1974
A thrilling run to Wembley in the FA Cup
ends in a defeat to Liverpool. 1975 Joe
Harvey steps aside and new manager Gordon
Lee arrives at Gallowgate.

Newcastle United's successful European squad with the Inter Cities Fairs Cup trophy. Back row, left to right: Burton, Foggon, Dave Smith (trainer), Clark, Ross. Middle row: McNamee, Craggs, Hope, McFaul, Gibb, Davies. Front row: Scott, Sinclair, Moncur, Joe Harvey (manager), Robson, Craig, Arentoft.

The cycle of football had turned again, and United's great 1950s' team eventually declined as the club fell from grace, dropping into the second tier of football. Old war-horse Joe Harvey was the man to remodel the Magpies. He first gained promotion, then guided the club into European competition for the first time – and won a trophy at the first attempt – before building an entertaining eleven full of sparkling names that took United back to Wembley. It was an era full of headlines and characters.

LEFT: Before European football took a grip on Tyneside, the region had to come to terms with relegation in 1961. Yet the hotbed of football remained as strong as ever. Kids knocked a ball around every street, here in the Scotswood area of the city.

ABOVE RIGHT: A new manager was needed and former skipper of the heady days of the Forties and Fifties, Joe Harvey returned in 1962 to rebuild the club. It was a popular move.

A new Breed Arrives

ABOVE: Harvey completely revamped the Magpies squad.
Many old-heads moved on, such as Mitchell, White and
McMichael, and a new breed arrived, some thoughtful
signings, others from the youth system. Included were

A new centre-forward arrived on Tyneside, Barrie Thomas, from Scunthorpe United. He was quite a goal-getter and scored no fewer than 41 goals in the 1961/2 season for his two clubs. Thomas was a live wire, erratic but ever dangerous. This spectacular action photograph sees Barrie flying in mid-air at St James' Park to reach a cross before George Curtis of Coventry City.

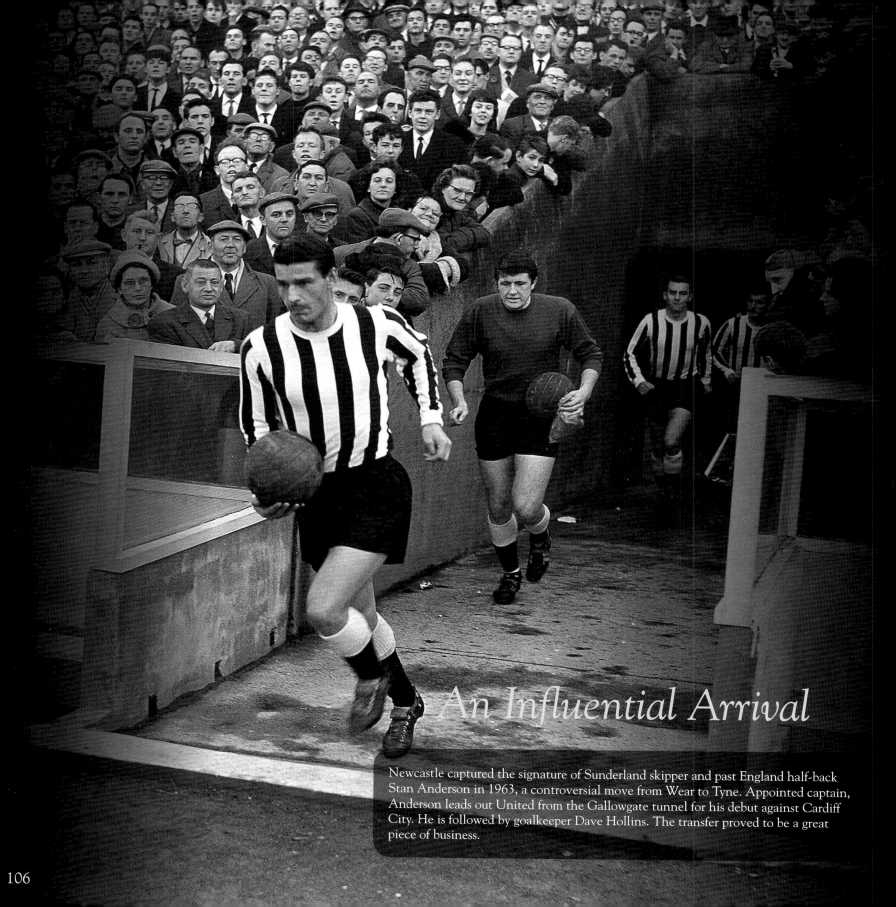

An Influential Arrival

Newcastle captured the signature of Sunderland skipper and past England half-back Stan Anderson in 1963, a controversial move from Wear to Tyne. Appointed captain, Anderson leads out United from the Gallowgate tunnel for his debut against Cardiff City. He is followed by goalkeeper Dave Hollins. The transfer proved to be a great piece of business.

The first stage of manager Joe Harvey's rebuilding of the Magpies was complete when United lifted the Second Division title and rejoined the elite of football in 1965. Harvey fashioned a tough and uncompromising eleven with a solid defence, all marshalled expertly by the experienced half-back line of Anderson, McGrath and Iley. United clinched promotion, similar to their achievements in 1948, with an Easter victory, 2-0 against rivals Bolton Wanderers on Tyneside. Almost 60,000 saw that triumph.

Record: P42 W24 D9 L9 F81 A45 – 57 Pts – Position 1st.
Regular side: Marshall, Craig, Clark, Anderson, McGrath, Iley, Hockey or Robson, Hilley, McGarry or Cummings, Penman, Suddick.
Top scorers: McGarry 16, Hilley 12.
Captain: Stan Anderson.
Manager: Joe Harvey.

Manager Joe Harvey (left) and captain Stan Anderson (right) proudly hold the Division Two Championship trophy with Chairman Lord Westwood behind. Westwood carried on the United tradition of prominent characters in the boardroom. The picture also captures a rare view of the now long gone Second Division trophy.

BACKGROUND: The Sixties and Seventies saw a generation of football fans brought up in the Newcastle United Kop – the Leazes End – located under a simple covered structure at the north end of the ground. Featured in the background to this United versus Liverpool clash, it was noisy, raucous and a touch rough: Moncur and Burton halt Kevin Keegan.

BELOW: Willie McFaul, a young Irish goalkeeper, was added to the squad in 1966, caught in spectacular action against Manchester City. He went on to appear on 355 occasions for the club and also served as both coach and manager.

WAGS – Sixties Style

The Sixties and Seventies were the days of the Beatles, Led Zeppelin, Carnaby Street and the mini-skirt. And by then some footballers WAGs had started to create publicity themselves. England skipper Billy Wright was married to one of the Beverley Sisters – the Spice Girls of the early Sixties. Two of United's players are pictured with their WAGs during the era.

LEFT: Jim Iley is caught at home with his wife, Lily, complete with Sixties-style coffee service and flamboyant curtains.

BACKGROUND: The period saw huge changes in society as the somewhat austere post-war years were swept away by pop music and psychedelic design. Bryan Robson is pictured with his girlfriend – and later wife – table-tennis champion Maureen Hepple.

A Record Signing on the Scene

Transfer fees escalated dramatically in the Sixties and were to jump even higher in the following decade. Newcastle were one of the big spenders again, paying a record £80,000 for Welsh international centre-forward Wyn Davies in 1966. In action against Chelsea (far right), the Mighty Wyn, as he was nicknamed, became something of a cult figure on Tyneside – and a key player in United's European triumph.

FAR LEFT: Newcastle were almost set for their European adventure. Tommy Gibb was another influential arrival, a bargain signing from Partick Thistle. With his endless stamina he was ideally suited for the engine-room of midfield.

LEFT: The emergence of Bryan Robson as a top striker was another significant factor in the Magpies resurgence. Nicknamed Pop, and at Gallowgate since a youngster in 1962, it was during the 1968/9 season that he flourished, with many judges wanting him in the England side.

ABOVE: The partnership up front of Wyn Davies (right) and Pop Robson (left) was hugely effective. Davies often caused panic and mayhem in the opposition box with his physical and aerial menace. Robson was on hand to capitalize. In Europe, continental defenders had no answer to the duo.

Fairs Cup Final 1969

Newcastle's two-legged clash with Hungarians Újpesti Dózsa proved to be a classic encounter. With United taking a comfortable three-goal advantage to Budapest, the Tynesiders faced a torrid first half and were on the rack by the break. Having conceded two goals the Magpies looked like being overrun by the experienced and fast-moving Eastern bloc side. But, inspired by what became a famous half-time team talk by boss Joe Harvey, Newcastle hit back to silence the crowd and regain the advantage. And it was skipper Bob Moncur who did the damage, netting the all-important away goal – his hat-trick over the two legs. It was enough to send United on their way to lift a first European trophy.

First leg:

Date & venue:	29th May 1969 at St James' Park. Newcastle United 3(0) Újpesti Dózsa 0(0).
United:	McFaul, Craig, Burton, Moncur, Clark, Scott, Gibb, Arentoft, Sinclair (Foggon), Robson, Davies.
Újpesti Dózsa:	Szentimihályi, Káposzta, Bánkuti, Dunai (E), Solymosi, Noskó, Fazekas, Göröcs, Bene, Dunai (A), Zámbó.
Goals:	United – Moncur (63m, 71m), Scott (84m).
Attendance:	59,234.

Second leg:

Date & venue:	11th June 1969 at Megyeri Stadion, Budapest. Newcastle United 3(0) Újpesti Dózsa 2(2) (Aggregate 6-2).
United:	McFaul, Craig, Burton, Moncur, Clark, Scott (Foggon), Gibb, Arentoft, Sinclair, Robson, Davies.
Újpesti Dózsa:	Szentimihályi, Káposzta, Bánkuti, Dunai (E), Solymosi, Noskó, Fazekas, Göröcs, Bene, Dunai (A), Zámbó.
Goals:	United – Moncur (46m), Arentoft (53m), Foggon (68m). Újpesti – Bene (30m), Göröcs (43m).
Attendance:	34,000.
Captain:	Bob Moncur.
Manager:	Joe Harvey.

> " *All you've got to do is score a goal. These foreigners are all the same, they'll collapse like a pack of cards.* "
>
> Joe Harvey

114

European excitement reached a frenzy as United took a 3-0 advantage after the first leg of the Fairs Cup final. Supporters in the near 60,000 crowd go wild as United score.

LEFT: Tyneside's public took to European football from the off, and St James' Park was more often than not a sell-out for three seasons of European action. The Fairs Cup final against Újpesti Dózsa on Tyneside was the first leg of a dramatic contest. Bryan Robson catches this effort sweetly on the volley.

OFFICIAL SOUVENIR PROGRAMME

PRICE 1/-

INTER CITIES FAIRS' CUP

FINAL TIE First Leg

Season 1968-69

No. 53

NEWCASTLE UNITED

ST. JAMES' PARK · NEWCASTLE UPON TYNE

versus

UJPEST DOZSA

THURSDAY, 29th MAY, 1969

KICK-OFF 7.30 p.m.

1969. június 11. ★ 20 óra
Megyeri úti Dózsa Stadion

ÚJPEST DÓZSA – NEWCASTLE UNITED

VVK-döntő

Ára: 2,— forint

Fairs Cup final programmes.

FAR LEFT: Newcastle United's squad received a rousing welcome inside St James' Park on a sun-drenched June afternoon. On the lap of honour Frank Clark hoists the trophy to the crowd. Bob Moncur is on hand too.

BELOW: An open-topped bus parade from Newcastle Airport to St James' Park took place as United's cup victors returned from Budapest. Bob Moncur shows off the trophy – now suitably decorated with a black-and-white scarf – alongside centre-half John McNamee.

Captain Bob – for Club and Country

> *He would be worth millions if he was playing now.*
>
> Terry McDermott

Bob Moncur leads out Scotland alongside Bobby Moore of England for the Auld Enemy clash at Wembley in 1971. A crowd of 100,000 saw the match end in a 3-1 English victory.

–LEGENDS–

Bob Moncur

A hero at the back… and up front
Captain of club and country, Bob Moncur became one of football's top defenders, a centre-half who was tough, commanding and could read the game. Arguably United's finest defender, he led the Magpies into European competition for the first time and duly lifted the Fairs Cup trophy in 1968/9, in the process netting a hat-trick in the two-legged final. An adopted Geordie, Moncur afterwards settled in the region, a popular and knowledgeable character on all things Newcastle United.

FOOTBALL –STATS–

Bob Moncur

Name: Robert Moncur

Born: Perth 1945

Playing Career: 1960–1977

Clubs: Newcastle United, Sunderland, Carlisle United

United League & Cup appearances: 346

United League & Cup goals: 8

Fairs Cup winner 1969, FA Cup finalist 1974, Division Two Champions 1965

Scotland appearances: 16

At home with the Moncurs, wife Camille and children. Bob remained on Tyneside after his footballing days, now a popular radio and television pundit.

119

The Adventure Continues – a Trip to Porto

ABOVE: Following United's opening success, the Black 'n' Whites were no longer dismissed as novices. They earned respect and continued to perform well, defeating amongst others the mighty Internazionale Milano. They also took care of FC Porto and a *Daily Mirror* photographer captured the trip to Portugal in 1969. United's party at the airport, left to right: Frank Clark, Ben Arentoft, Bob Moncur, Ollie Burton and Pop Robson.

RIGHT: Newcastle's squad get a feel for the vast Estádio das Antas bowl in Porto. Manager Joe Harvey (centre) is flanked by coach Dave Smith (left) and Ollie Burton.

LEFT: The tie with FC Porto resulted in a tough and close match, but United came back from Portugal with a satisfactory 0-0 draw, eventually winning with a single goal at St James' Park. Pictured is Tommy Gibb going past two Porto defenders.

RIGHT: Keith Dyson, a product of United's flourishing youth system, hailed from County Durham and was given some rough treatment up front. He was at one stage carried off by Porto players, with Wyn Davies in attendance.

A Change in Strategy

With United's European adventure coming to a close in 1971, boss Joe Harvey opted for a makeover to his Magpie side. Newcastle's manager decided on a change in strategy, bringing in a group of entertaining stars and personalities. Record signing Malcolm Macdonald led the way, alongside the likes of Jimmy Smith, Terry Hibbitt, Tony Green and a young, promising midfielder, Terry McDermott. It brought a period of thrill-a-minute football, and another FA Cup final.

Joe Harvey broke Newcastle's transfer record making Aberdeen's Scottish international playmaker Jimmy Smith the club's first six-figure buy when he paid a reported £100,000 in 1969. Although inconsistent, Jinky, as he was known, delighted supporters with his skills.

ABOVE: Up front Newcastle's boss broke the bank again with £180,000 to make sure the Second Division goalscoring machine Malcolm Macdonald pulled on a black-and-white shirt. His first senior appearance at Gallowgate was sensational – rattling in a hat-trick against Liverpool in August 1971. Macdonald fires across goalkeeper Ray Clemence and into the net.

RIGHT: Supermac had arrived. He acclaims the crowd, hugged by Terry Hibbitt.

Here Comes Supermac

No. 9 Heroes

Since very earliest times, Newcastle United have enjoyed a tradition of fielding a *Roy of the Rovers* type centre-forward, and now the club's impressive list of No. 9 Heroes is something of a legend in the game. The rapport that has developed over the years between centre-forward and supporter can be found nowhere else in the country. It all started with Peddie, Appleyard and Shepherd in the early years, then Neil Harris, Hughie Gallacher and Jack Allen to the wartime exploits of Albert Stubbins. Then came Wor Jackie Milburn, Len White and Wyn Davies, to Malcolm Macdonald – Supermac to all – Mirandinha, Mick Quinn and modern-day goalscoring icons Andy Cole, Les Ferdinand and of course Alan Shearer. All are now part of Tyneside folklore.

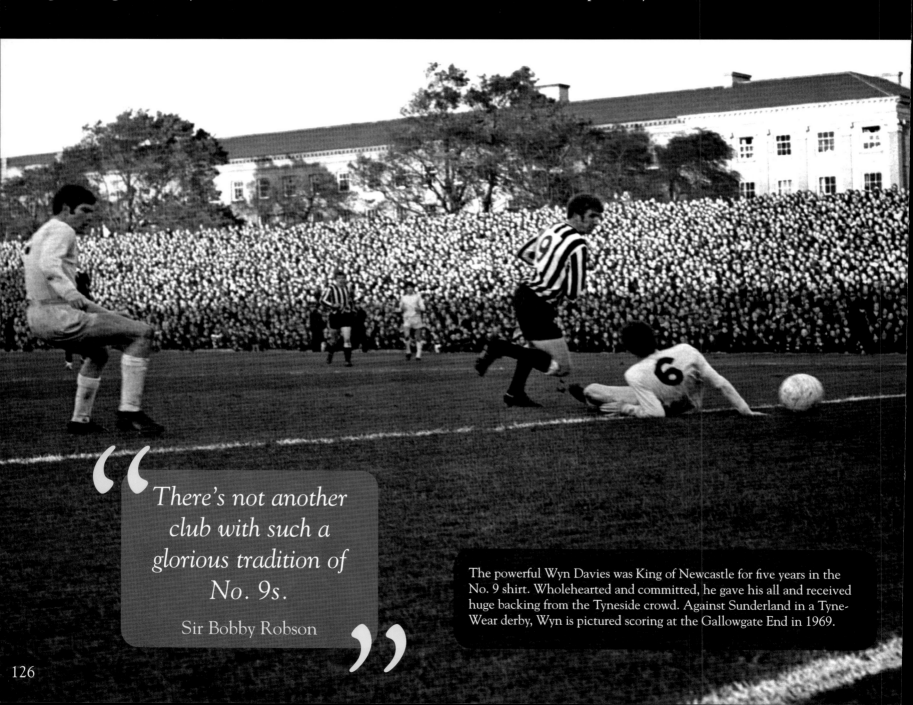

> *There's not another club with such a glorious tradition of No. 9s.*
>
> Sir Bobby Robson

The powerful Wyn Davies was King of Newcastle for five years in the No. 9 shirt. Wholehearted and committed, he gave his all and received huge backing from the Tyneside crowd. Against Sunderland in a Tyne-Wear derby, Wyn is pictured scoring at the Gallowgate End in 1969.

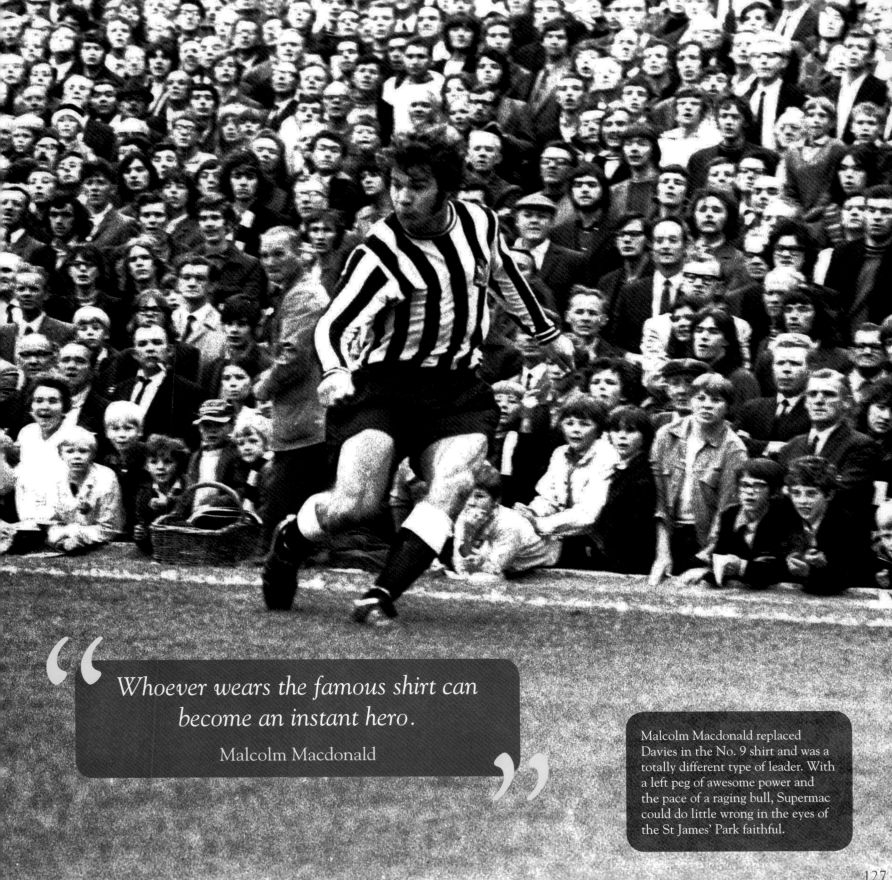

> *Whoever wears the famous shirt can become an instant hero.*
>
> Malcolm Macdonald

Malcolm Macdonald replaced Davies in the No. 9 shirt and was a totally different type of leader. With a left peg of awesome power and the pace of a raging bull, Supermac could do little wrong in the eyes of the St James' Park faithful.

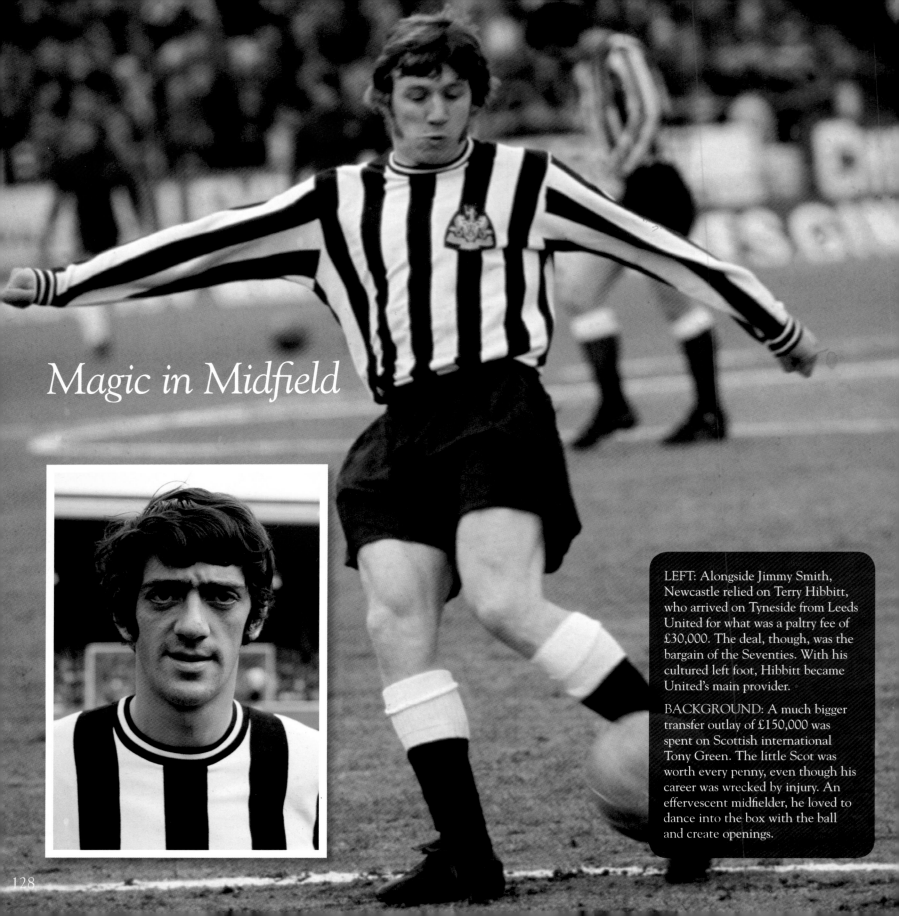

Magic in Midfield

LEFT: Alongside Jimmy Smith, Newcastle relied on Terry Hibbitt, who arrived on Tyneside from Leeds United for what was a paltry fee of £30,000. The deal, though, was the bargain of the Seventies. With his cultured left foot, Hibbitt became United's main provider.

BACKGROUND: A much bigger transfer outlay of £150,000 was spent on Scottish international Tony Green. The little Scot was worth every penny, even though his career was wrecked by injury. An effervescent midfielder, he loved to dance into the box with the ball and create openings.

Giant-killing Victims

Newcastle United have a proud tradition in the FA Cup, reaching no fewer than 13 finals, six times as victors. However, in the true romance of the competition, the Magpies have more than once also suffered at the hands of the football minnow. In pre-war seasons they were knocked out by then non-league sides Southampton St Mary's (1898 and 1900) and Crystal Palace (1907). It was more recently, though, when United created two of the biggest upsets in the tournament's history. During 1964 little Bedford Town arrived on Tyneside and defeated the six-times FA Cup winners 2-1. Then in 1972 Hereford United claimed a draw at Gallowgate and famously won the replay by the same 2-1 scoreline – all with the BBC in attendance to film the event for posterity – and to the recurring torment of all Geordies.

Edgar Street, Hereford in 1972. The now famous venue for the giant-killing feat of the era, United's exit at the hands of non-league Hereford United. Ricky George (white shirt, centre) shoots low past Willie McFaul to grab the winner.

129

–LEGENDS–

Malcolm Macdonald

Supermac to all on Tyneside

A match-winning No. 9 striker who possessed shooting power and pace like few before or after. Swashbuckling, brash and arrogant on and off the field, United's supporters took to him from the very start and an enduring bond formed which lasted long after he headed south for Highbury. Macdonald scored many a goal in a breathtaking and exciting manner; he was the focal point of United's side for five years during the Seventies.

FOOTBALL –STATS–

Malcolm Macdonald

Name: Malcolm Ian Macdonald

Born: Fulham 1950

Playing Career: 1967–1979

Clubs: Fulham, Luton Town, Newcastle United, Arsenal, Djurgardens (loan)

United League & Cup appearances: 228

United League & Cup goals: 121

FA Cup finalist 1974, League Cup finalist 1976

England appearances: 14

LEFT: Goals were what Malcolm Macdonald lived for. Apart from bagging over 120 for United, he also once netted all five for England at Wembley against Cyprus in 1975.

ABOVE: Malcolm Macdonald was a dedicated follower of fashion. Indeed, he opened a boutique in Newcastle during his time at St James' Park. Mac never lost his love for the region, returning to live on Tyneside.

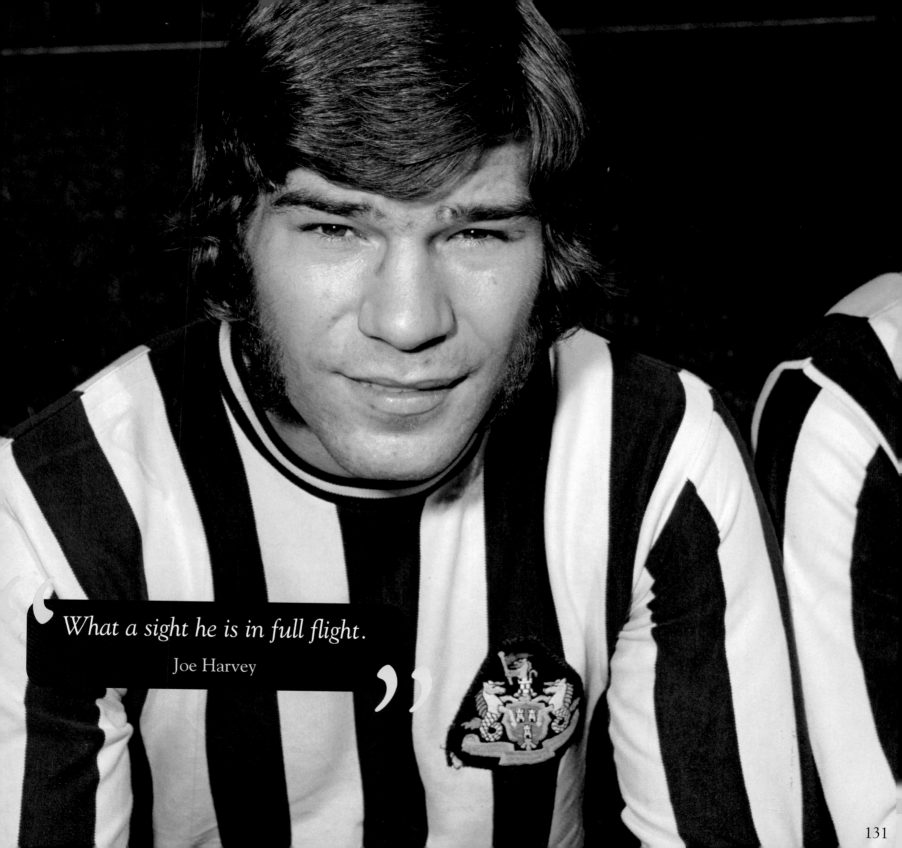

> *What a sight he is in full flight.*
>
> Joe Harvey

LEFT: While there were plenty of new faces at Gallowgate, Joe Harvey retained some old favourites. David Craig was one, at the club since 1960. He was rated as one of the top right-backs in the country, here against George Armstrong of Arsenal. Craig totalled 412 games for the club over 15 seasons.

ABOVE: Another talented midfield creator was Tommy Cassidy, who developed from a raw Irish youngster into an international player good enough to shine in the World Cup finals of 1982.

Welsh international centre-half Ollie Burton (left) and Terry Hibbitt (right) pose for the camera. Hibbitt has all the football accessories of the day — extra wide lapels on a trendy jacket and a flowery, colourful shirt and tie.

133

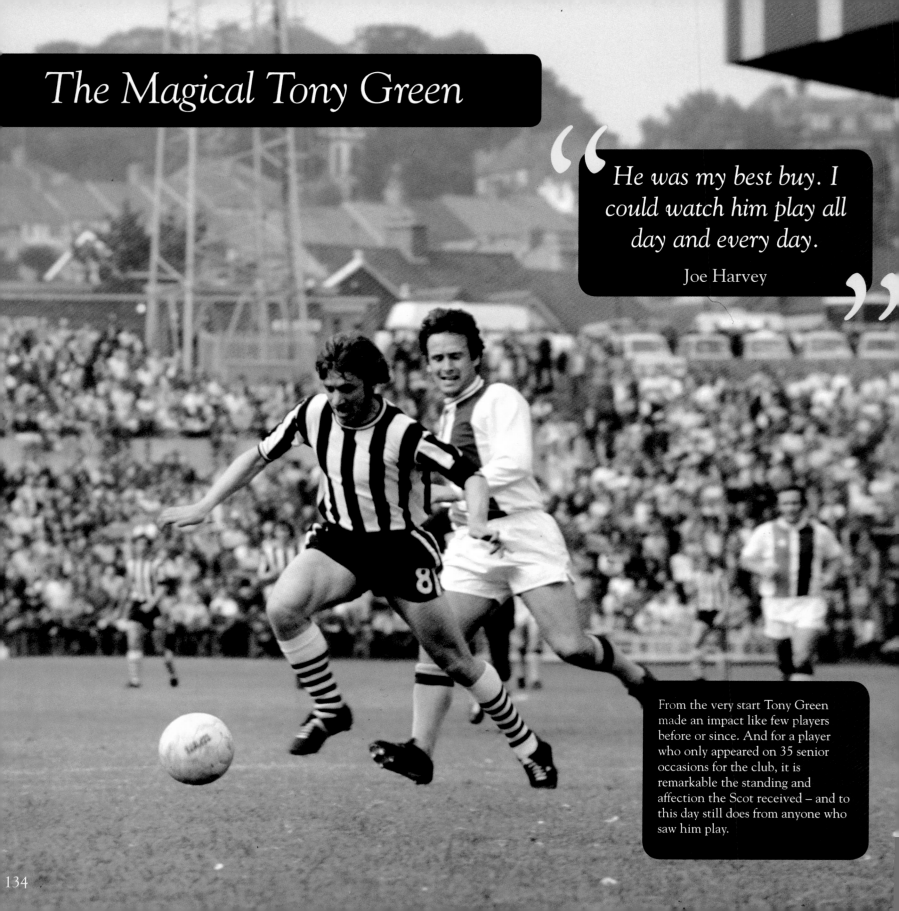

The Magical Tony Green

He was my best buy. I could watch him play all day and every day.

Joe Harvey

From the very start Tony Green made an impact like few players before or since. And for a player who only appeared on 35 senior occasions for the club, it is remarkable the standing and affection the Scot received – and to this day still does from anyone who saw him play.

A Career Ruined at....Crystal Palace

Green's career was ruined. Tony retired in December 1973 and took up a new life in teaching. A huge talent was lost to football.

The Palace jinx returned in September 1972 when Green was scythed down at Selhurst Park by Crystal Palace defender Mel Blyth and seriously damaged his knee. He was stretchered off and out of football for over a year.

The Age of the Hooligan

The late 1960s and 1970s saw a huge upsurge in football hooliganism across England and Scotland. The police had a tough job in trying to control the largely unsegregated terracing on every ground in the country, and when English and Scottish clubs met, either in so-called friendlies or in European ties, all hell was unleashed.

LEFT: When Glasgow Rangers faced United in the Fairs Cup semi-final of 1969 mayhem reigned over Tyneside. The same happened in a supposed friendly encounter at St James' Park during 1968 with the other half of the Glasgow Old Firm, Celtic. Police escort two Glaswegians – fuelled by drink and worse for wear – out of the stadium.

TOP RIGHT: Trouble on the streets of Newcastle when Sunderland arrived in the city during the 1970s. Mounted police restore order while a police dog takes a tasty bite of one fan's trouser leg!

RIGHT: Gradually control was regained within the stadiums. At St James' Park a huge police presence was needed for some while – and they had their own mini-stools to enjoy the action!

137

On the Wembley Trail Again

Joe Harvey's entertaining side reached Wembley in 1974 and, as ever, the FA Cup run was a thrilling roller-coaster. A quarter-final with Nottingham Forest became a controversial tie, United winning 4-3 – with John Tudor heading a brilliant goal – before the FA ordered a replay due to a pitch invasion.

Action at Hillsborough in the Semi-final

ABOVE: Newcastle's meeting with Burnley at Hillsborough in the FA Cup semi-final of 1974 has gone down in the annals as Supermac's finest hour. But the other hero of the match was Terry Hibbitt, Supermac's feeder in midfield. Terry is in combat with Burnley's Frank Casper. Frank Clark looks on.

RIGHT: Supermac's second half double at Hillsborough was stunning. Both goals were breakaway chases, with Macdonald's pace and power outstripping defenders. His cool finish on both occasions had 30,000 Geordie fans in raptures of delight. This is his first strike, sliding the ball past goalkeeper Stevenson.

141

Wembley Revisited

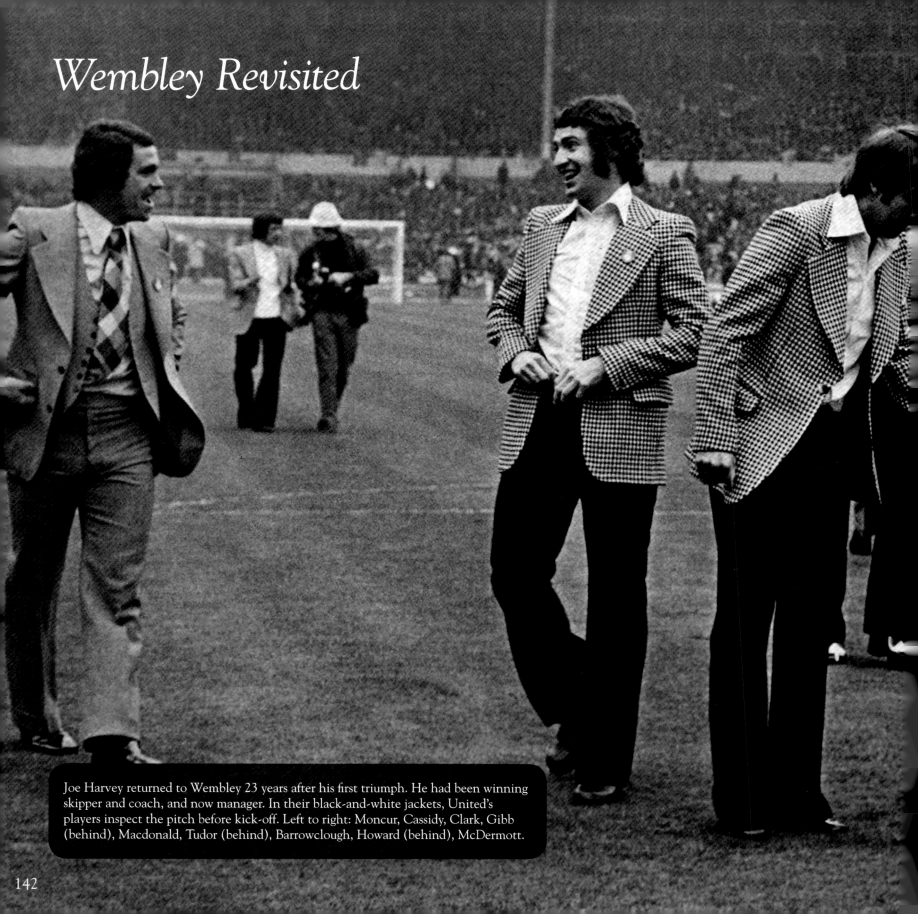

Joe Harvey returned to Wembley 23 years after his first triumph. He had been winning skipper and coach, and now manager. In their black-and-white jackets, United's players inspect the pitch before kick-off. Left to right: Moncur, Cassidy, Clark, Gibb (behind), Macdonald, Tudor (behind), Barrowclough, Howard (behind), McDermott.

FA Cup Final 1974

It was United's first domestic final for almost 20 years, yet after such an exhilarating FA Cup run to Wembley, the big day in London was a huge let-down. And it was a Tyneside hero of the future who was largely to spoil the Geordies' day out, a certain Kevin Keegan. Following a drab first half, Liverpool stepped up a gear: Keegan scored their first goal and set the course for the outcome. Newcastle never looked like getting back into the contest, and the Merseysiders completely swamped United by the end of the match.

Date & venue:	4th May 1974 at Wembley Stadium. Newcastle United 0(0) Liverpool 3(0).
United:	McFaul, Clark, Howard, Moncur, Kennedy, McDermott, Smith (Gibb), Cassidy, Hibbitt, Tudor, Macdonald.
Liverpool:	Clemence, Smith, Thompson, Hughes, Lindsay, Cormack, Hall, Callaghan, Heighway, Toshack, Keegan.
Goals:	Liverpool – Keegan (58m, 88m), Heighway (75m).
Attendance:	100,000.
Captain:	Bob Moncur.
Manager:	Joe Harvey.

> *This final will haunt me for ever.*
>
> Joe Harvey

LEFT: Referee Gordon Kew brings the two captains together before the start of the contest, Bob Moncur (left) and Liverpool's Emlyn Hughes (right).

BACKGROUND: Newcastle United flopped badly at Wembley and had to watch a slick Liverpool side dominate most of the match. Kevin Keegan, pictured in the final, destroyed the club he was to have such an association with in the future.

FOOTBALL ASSOCIATION CHALLENGE
CUP COMPETITION

FINAL

LIVERPOOL

NEWCASTLE
UNITED

F.A. CUP HONOURS
WINNERS
1965
Runners-up
1914, 1950, 1971

F.A. CUP HONOURS
WINNERS
1910, 1924, 1932,
1951, 1952, 1955
Runners-up
1905, 1906, 1908,
1911

SATURDAY, 4th MAY 1974
Kick-off 3 p.m.

OFFICIAL
PROGRAMME

WEMBLEY
STADIUM

FIFTEEN
PENCE

1974 FA Cup final programme.

Not a Superday for Supermac

Much was expected of Malcolm Macdonald at Wembley, but it proved to be 90 minutes his colleagues and everyone from Tyneside wanted to quickly forget.

Toon Army – '70s Style

There were plenty of black-and-white flags and scarves in evidence
during the Seventies, with United's massive army of support as
fervent then as now. But 35 years ago there were also flares on the
trousers, flowers on the shirts and hair galore, whiskers and all.
Known then as "the Black 'n' White Army" rather than the Toon
Army, the terrace chant was 'Howay The Lads... Howay The Lads!'.

What a Welcome for a Defeated Team!

Although the Magpies had performed poorly at Wembley and let down their huge following, an incredible welcome home awaited the squad as they returned from Wembley – a defeated team. St James' Park was full – the only thing that was missing was the FA Cup.

LEFT: The Black 'n' White Army of the Seventies travelled the country following their heroes – and were as colourful and noisy as they are today. Pictured in full song at the Leazes End at St James' Park, a local policeman is keen to make sure he gets in the frame.

ABOVE: Not a winning FA Cup procession through the streets but a losing one. Yet supporters were still keen to show their support in adversity – and appreciation of what had been a thrill-a-minute cup run in 1973/4.

151

Revolution on Tyne
1975-1993

Newcastle United's relative success as the club moved into the modern world of football revolved around one personality – Kevin Keegan, first as a player, then as a manager. He forged a quite remarkable bond with the Tyneside public.

> " *We need a result, but we'll get it, survive and take off.*
>
> Kevin Keegan "

1976 United's first Football League Cup final ends in a defeat to Manchester City. **1977** Gordon Lee departs and Richard Dinnis takes over, yet United qualify for Europe. **1978** Internal turmoil leads to a disastrous season and United drop into Division Two. **1979** With Bill McGarry in charge, United attempt to bounce back but finish in 8th place. **1980** Failure in a promotion challenge again, knocked out by Sunderland in the League Cup. **1981** Arthur Cox takes control and starts to rebuild a new side, including Chris Waddle. **1982** England skipper Kevin Keegan sensationally arrives at St James' Park to a fanfare. **1983** Newcastle make headlines again but just fail in securing a promotion place. **1984** With Keegan, Beardsley and Waddle in harness, United gain promotion in style. **1985** Geordie hero Jack Charlton takes charge, United consolidate in Division One. **1986** Willie McFaul takes over and settles the camp after managerial turmoil. **1987** Peter Beardsley leaves for Anfield in a record £1.9 million deal. **1988** With Brazilian Mirandinha in the No. 9 shirt, United finish in 8th spot. **1989** Newcastle finish rock bottom in Division One and tumble back to football's second tier. **1990** United narrowly fail to gain promotion, falling in the play-offs to rivals Sunderland. **1991** Ossie Ardiles becomes boss as behind the scenes a share-war for the club begins. **1992** John Hall wins control of United and Kevin Keegan returns to become manager. **1993** Newcastle cruise to the First Division title and the Entertainers are born.

The 1980s was to see a brilliant trio of Geordies develop in a black-and-white shirt: Chris Waddle (pictured) along with Peter Beardsley and Paul Gascoigne. All became England regulars.

To the Modern Era

The relatively modern era of football up to the creation of the Premier League saw Newcastle United struggle, at first with how to come to terms with a rapidly developing football business, and then with how to find the right manager to bring what was becoming a sleeping-giant back with the best. As a consequence of unacceptable mediocrity, a revolution swept through St James' Park as the old guard ownership of the club was replaced by a dynamic new breed of football management and the financial muscle that came with it. This brought a return of Kevin Keegan as manager – the Messiah to lead the Toon into the new world of the Premiership.

> *People keep on about stars and flair. As far as I am concerned, you find stars in the sky and flair is something at the bottom of trousers.*
>
> Gordon Lee

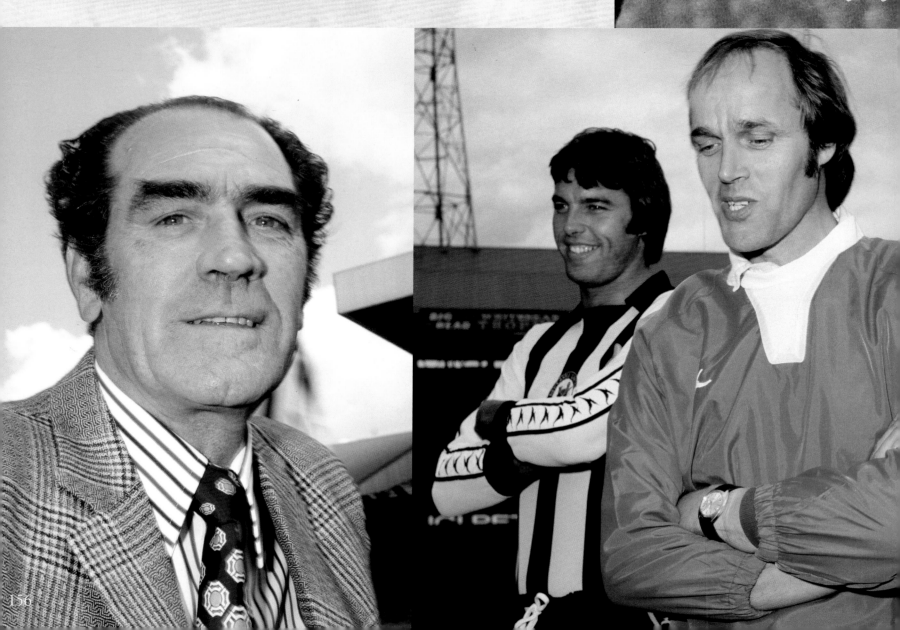

LEFT: Out went the old, in came the new. Loyal servant for over 35 years, Joe Harvey (left) moved upstairs during the close season of 1975 and the largely unheard of Gordon Lee (right) breezed into St James' Park. Out also went Newcastle's star system: the newborn Newcastle United was to be based upon team ethics and solid, hard work. Another Wembley appearance soon followed, so did a return to Europe, but then Newcastle collapsed dramatically, like the proverbial deck of cards – and they were back in Division Two.

BACKGROUND: Gordon Lee's side had a different make-up and several new faces. Centre-half Glenn Keeley, a Harvey signing, impressed at times. Here he gets a talking to from the referee in a clash with West Ham United.

157

United's First Football League Cup Final

"
We played well. We can go back to
Newcastle with our heads held high.

Gordon Lee
"

It took United almost 16 years to make an impression on the Football League Cup tournament since it started during 1960. The Magpies reached the final in 1976, Gordon Lee with stand-in captain Tommy Craig led United out at Wembley in their red track-

With United's squad hit by a flu bug in the
week before the final, the Magpies under the
circumstances performed to credit and gave
City a tough game at Wembley. Although Peter
Barnes gave them the lead early into the game,
Newcastle hit back and thoroughly deserved their
equalizer following a move between twin strikers
Macdonald and Gowling. Newcastle-born Dennis
Tueart grabbed what was the winner for City with
a spectacular overhead kick just after the break. It
was a goal fitting to win any final.

Date & venue: 28ᵗʰ February 1976 at Wembley Stadium.
Newcastle United 1(1) Manchester City 2(1).

United: Mahoney, Nattrass, Keeley, Howard, Kennedy,
Barrowclough, Burns, Cassidy, Craig (T), Gowling,
Macdonald.

Manchester City: Corrigan, Keegan, Doyle, Watson, Donnachie, Oakes,
Booth, Hartford, Barnes, Royle, Tueart.

Goals: United – Gowling (35m), City – Barnes (11m),
Tueart (46m).

Attendance: 100,000.
Captain: Tommy Craig.
Manager: Gordon Lee.

Football League Cup final programme.

Gowling, a former Manchester United striker, joined United at the beginning of the season from lower division football with Huddersfield Town. He resurrected his career with 30 goals for the Magpies in that 1975/6 campaign.

There was one moment of joy for United's travelling masses when Alan Gowling stabbed home the ball past City's goalkeeper Joe Corrigan to level the contest at 1-1.

A Goal fit to Win any Trophy

There was plenty of media attention before the final surrounding City's Geordie striker Dennis Tueart. And it just had to be Tueart who stole the show, netting the winner with this spectacular overhead kick. Watching helplessly are United's Micky Burns (No. 7 shirt), Tommy Craig (centre) and Glenn Keeley.

He is wearing a black and white shirt, he was born in the heart of Newcastle – but Dennis Tueart is not a United player and was Manchester City's Geordie hero at Wembley.

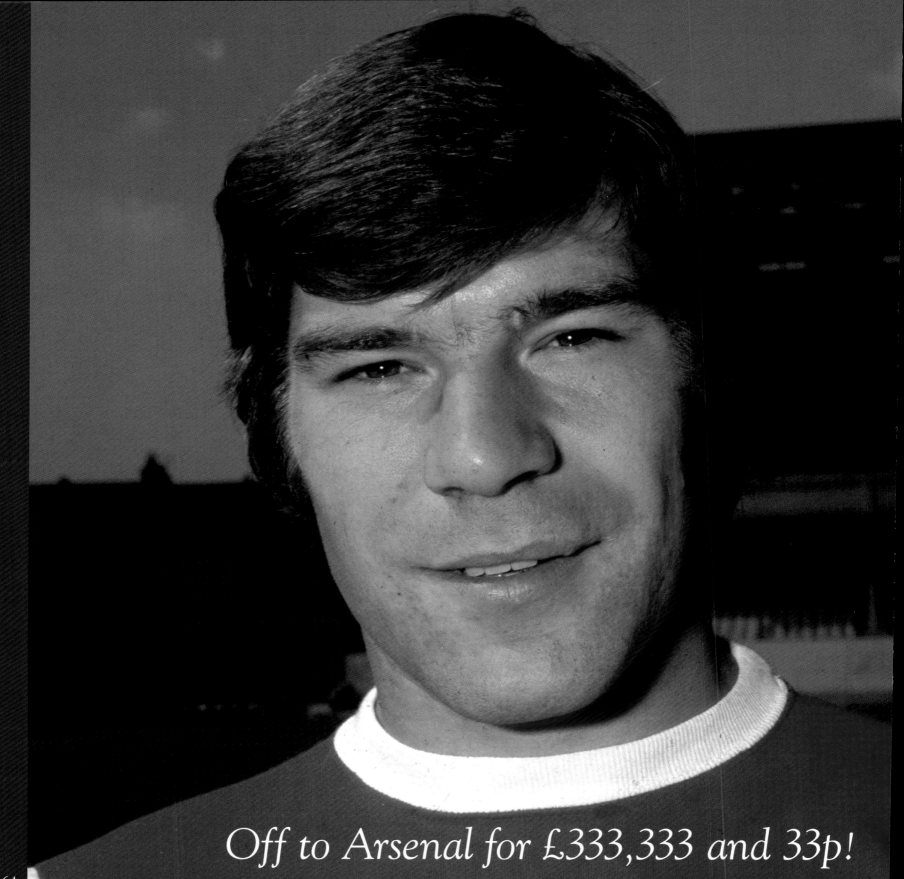

Off to Arsenal for £333,333 and 33p!

It was no surprise when crowd favourite Malcolm Macdonald headed south for Arsenal at the end of the 1975/6 season. He never got on with boss Gordon Lee and found the marble corridors of Highbury more to his liking.

> *I loved Newcastle until Gordon Lee took over.*
>
> Malcolm Macdonald

Manager Gordon Lee (far right) stops for the camera along with his players – minus Malcolm Macdonald – before an away trip. Lee himself was soon to depart, to Everton. Also featured is his assistant Richard Dinnis, who was to take over the manager's role in February 1977 and guide United back into Europe. Left to right: Ray Blackhall, Aidan McCaffery, Ray Hudson, Richard Dinnis, Alan Kennedy, Alan Guy and Gordon Lee. Behind are Graham Oates, David McLean and Irving Nattrass.

Two Full-backs of Quality

LEFT: Newcastle United have long held a tradition of fielding sound and capable home-grown full-backs. They produced two exceptional backs during this era, one of whom, Irving Nattrass, is pictured ready for a training session.

RIGHT: Alan Kennedy joined Nattrass on United's team-sheet. His attacking flair was eyecatching, going on to win top honours with Liverpool and twice hitting the goal that won the Reds the European Cup.

All Change

During the Eighties, manager after manager tried to give United stability and although the Black 'n' Whites created plenty of headlines as normal – including the sensational deal that brought England skipper Kevin Keegan to Tyneside – the club struggled to find the right blend on the pitch and come to terms with a new commercial world of football. Bill McGarry made way for Arthur Cox who, with Keegan as his talisman, got United promoted, then Jack Charlton briefly took the helm followed by Willie McFaul, Jim Smith – the Bald Eagle – and Ossie Ardiles. Gallowgate was a melting pot of Toon politics – all to end in rebellion and revolt.

RIGHT: Following the controversy of Gordon Lee's defection to Merseyside and the brief Dinnis regime, in November 1977 United turned to an experienced head to steady the rocky ship – former England wing-half and ex-Wolves boss, Bill McGarry.

LEFT: McGarry was a tough disciplinarian of the old school. But he could not halt the drop into football's second tier in the 1977/8 season. Sporting a distinctive chequered suit (left), he took his squad to Sweden to prepare for a promotion push.

Peter Withe (left) fell out with the sometimes controversial Brian Clough (right) at Nottingham Forest and moved north to Tyneside in 1978. It was a huge coup for McGarry, the centre-forward dropping a division to sign for the Magpies for a new club record fee of £200,000.

Strong and powerful, Withe needed a quick return to the top flight if he was to remain on Tyneside long.

The Little and Large Show

Peter Withe found the perfect foil in diminutive non-league star Alan Shoulder, who exchanged Blyth Spartans and a career in the pit to become United's new local hero. It was like *The Little and Large Show*, and for two seasons the partnership brought 59 goals. Shoulder is featured scoring a penalty against Oldham Athletic in 1979, Mick Martin watches.

Zico in the Snow

Never mind the famous Brazilian Zico who starred in the 1978 World Cup, United had their own Zico in midfield – Dubliner Mick Martin, pictured in the snow with his two daughters. Mick was nicknamed Zico after his driving runs from midfield for United.

Another Irishman, John Anderson, was as popular as Martin. Signed on a free transfer from Preston North End, John showed a never-say-die spirit as full-back, centre-half or in midfield, and went on to appear for the club on 332 occasions. He is pictured in action against Manchester City.

LEFT: Arthur Cox soon replaced Bill McGarry as boss in 1980 and brought Londoner Glenn Roeder to Tyneside to take control of his defence. Skilled and thoughtful at the back and popular with supporters, he later returned to the club, eventually taking charge himself.

LEFT: Born in the region, John Trewick became United's most expensive player at £250,000 when he returned to the North East from West Bromwich Albion. A good link-man in midfield, he performed well as the Black 'n' Whites headed for promotion.

BACKGROUND: Imre Varadi, in action against Barnsley, was United's goal threat for two seasons. Lively in attack, Varadi became a favourite and went on to score 42 goals before being controversially discarded.

> "We're in Heaven…We've Got Kevin.
>
> Russell Cushing"

BACKGROUND: Football fever hit Tyneside as England skipper Kevin Keegan joined the Magpies just before the start of the 1982/3 season. The country's biggest name, he single-handedly rejuvenated a slumbering football giant, Newcastle United.

LEFT: With family roots in the North East, Keegan declared he wanted to finish his playing career by leading the Magpies to promotion. Pictured with boss Arthur Cox the day he signed for United, crowds packed into every ground to see what became a Kevin Keegan bandwagon.

Arthur Cox (right) and Kevin Keegan (left) were the men to plot United's promotion. They missed out at the first attempt in 1982/3, but both men were doubly determined next time around.

Newcastle's public were caught up with the Keegan phenomenon. Interest was rekindled and tickets home and away were hard to find. And when United faced Liverpool in the FA Cup demand was huge. Note the Edwardian West Stand in the background.

Keegan returned to Anfield in January 1984 for that FA Cup pairing and received a warm welcome – but also a 4-0 football lesson. Pictured is Keegan with ex-United full-back Alan Kennedy.

Terry and Davie Mac Join the Bandwagon

Promotion 1984

Kevin Keegan's high-profile finale as a player was crowned with United's promotion back to Division One. With an attacking flair that has been matched since only by Keegan's side as a manager, Newcastle stormed into a promotion place in style, through the goal threat up front of Keegan as well as two emerging Geordie strikers, Peter Beardsley and Chris Waddle. A magical 4-0 home victory over Derby County all but assured their promotion, but a point at Huddersfield made absolutely sure.

Record: P42 W24 D8 L10 F85 A53 – 80 Pts – Position 3rd.
Regular side: Thomas or Carr, Anderson, Carney, Roeder, Ryan or Wharton, McCreery, McDermott, Wharton or Trewick, Beardsley, Keegan, Waddle.
Top scorers: Keegan 27, Beardsley 20, Waddle 18.
Captain: Kevin Keegan.
Manager: Arthur Cox.

FAR LEFT: Experienced internationals, Northern Ireland's David McCreery (above) and England's Terry McDermott (below) marshalled United's midfield.

BACKGROUND: Pictured against Oldham, Terry McDermott had been at United before, joining the club in 1973 and making a name before moving to Liverpool. In the coming years he was to become assistant to Keegan as manager and also to Kenny Dalglish, Graeme Souness and Glenn Roeder. Note the crowd fencing, in place for several seasons at the time in a bid to halt hooliganism spilling onto the pitch.

RIGHT: Kevin Keegan skippered United back to top-flight football – and led from the front with 27 goals (28 league and cup). His awareness and clinical finishing stood out. Pictured celebrating one of those goals, notice more crowd fencing, this time at Craven Cottage.

LEFT: Promotion celebrations in full swing at Gallowgate after the final game of the programme against Brighton during May 1984. Kevin Keegan leads the party, following a season of scintillating football for the purist.

TOP LEFT: John Anderson, wearing a fan's bowler, looking emotionally drained by the occasion.

BACKGROUND: United's players pay homage to their marvellous support. Left to right: John Trewick, Steve Carney, Chris Waddle, Kevin Keegan, Terry McDermott and goalkeeper Kevin Carr.

Joy on Tyneside...
The Toon are Back with the Best

Geordie Boys

Local heroes take the stage

During the Eighties Newcastle produced three players of exceptional talent, all to become worldwide stars of football: Peter Beardsley, Chris Waddle and Paul Gascoigne. This trio of Geordie boys made their name in a black-and-white shirt and thrilled the Tyneside crowd before moving on for big fees to clubs who could fulfil their ambition at the time. All three were crowd-pleasers of the highest quality, and one, Peter Beardsley, returned to St James' Park to almost skipper the side to the Premiership title in 1996. Another local hero was to join him – a certain Alan Shearer.

> *Waddle was a scorer of great goals… and developed into a fantastic player.*
>
> Peter Beardsley

–LEGENDS–

Chris Waddle

A match-winner on the wing

United took something of a gamble when they plucked Chris Waddle from Tow Law Town in local Northern League football. He was a raw, outside-left who had much to learn, but who also possessed untapped ability on the ball to win a game. Gradually that special talent developed – rapidly so under the influence of Kevin Keegan – and Chris eventually became an England regular. With his own unique style, Waddle could glide past defenders and whip a dangerous ball into the danger area, while he also often scored himself from weaving runs or curling free-kicks.

FOOTBALL –STATS–

Chris Waddle

Name: Christopher Roland Waddle

Born: Gateshead 1960

Playing Career: 1978–1998

Clubs: Newcastle United, Tottenham Hotspur, Marseille, Sheffield Wednesday, Falkirk, Bradford City, Sunderland, Burnley, Torquay United

United League & Cup appearances: 191

United League & Cup goals: 52

England appearances: 62

LEFT: Waddle was not just a winger who could leave his full-back for dead. As captured by this picture against Rotherham, he often cut inside and was able to find the net.

TOP RIGHT: England beckoned for the Tynesider once he tasted life in the top flight.

BACKGROUND: A swerve one way, a jink the other, and Chris Waddle rides the tackle of a Barnsley defender in 1981. His natural talent blossomed during the 1983/4 season, with Kevin Keegan alongside.

All Change at Gallowgate – Again

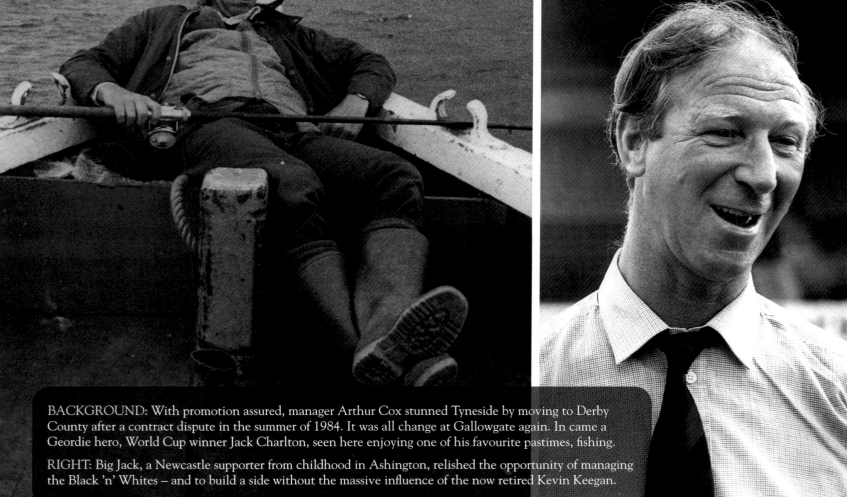

BACKGROUND: With promotion assured, manager Arthur Cox stunned Tyneside by moving to Derby County after a contract dispute in the summer of 1984. It was all change at Gallowgate again. In came a Geordie hero, World Cup winner Jack Charlton, seen here enjoying one of his favourite pastimes, fishing.

RIGHT: Big Jack, a Newcastle supporter from childhood in Ashington, relished the opportunity of managing the Black 'n' Whites – and to build a side without the massive influence of the now retired Kevin Keegan.

Big Jack's Twin Strike Force

ABOVE RIGHT: Charlton had the rapidly developing talents of Peter Beardsley and Chris Waddle as the cornerstone of his team, but he also decided upon a change in playing style. He brought in two tall strikers to compete up front, George Reilly and Tony Cunningham. At 6ft 4in tall, Reilly – pictured with Liverpool's Bruce Grobbelaar – was soon nicknamed Rambo.

BACKGROUND: Pictured against Chelsea, Tony Cunningham was 6ft 2in tall and another centre-forward who wanted the ball in the air more often than not. The problem for Jack Charlton was that neither Waddle nor Beardsley liked the different approach – nor did United's support.

–LEGENDS–

Peter Beardsley

An inspiration to all

A Newcastle supporter as a lad, it took Peter Beardsley a long route – via Carlisle and Vancouver – to pull on the black-and-white shirt, but then he had two rewarding spells at St James' Park. Having a special bond with Kevin Keegan, first as a player, then as a manager, Beardsley was a striker who kept fans on the edge of their seats. Yet he was also a team-player and incessant worker for the cause, and, importantly he could win a match with a dazzling run, slice of magic, or thundering shot. Rarely did he net the proverbial tap-in, though he usually provided the encore.

FOOTBALL –STATS–

Peter Beardsley

Name: Peter Andrew Beardsley MBE

Born: Newcastle upon Tyne 1961

Playing Career: 1979–1999

Clubs: Carlisle United, Vancouver Whitecaps, Manchester United (loan), Newcastle United, Liverpool, Everton, Newcastle United (again), Bolton Wanderers, Manchester City (loan), Fulham, Hartlepool United

United League & Cup appearances: 324

United League & Cup goals: 119

England appearances: 59

ABOVE: Alongside Chris Waddle, fellow Tynesider Peter Beardsley also developed as a special talent. A little genius in attack or midfield, now in the First Division, his career took off.

LEFT: Peter receiving the North East Sports Personality of the Year award at Newcastle Civic Centre from HRH Prince Philip in 1987. There were plenty more honours to follow for Beardsley.

> "Peter was a little maestro, pure and simple."
>
> Sir Bobby Robson

Beardsley was also soon in the England side and was to form a productive pairing with Gary Lineker during the World Cup of 1986 under Bobby Robson. He is pictured here giving a Paraguay defender a problem or two.

During the 1980s the club began to use their St James' Park arena for prestige music concerts. First to arrive were the Rolling Stones in 1982, then Bob Dylan, followed by Bruce Spingsteen in June 1985. The Boss is pictured playing at a packed Gallowgate above and left.

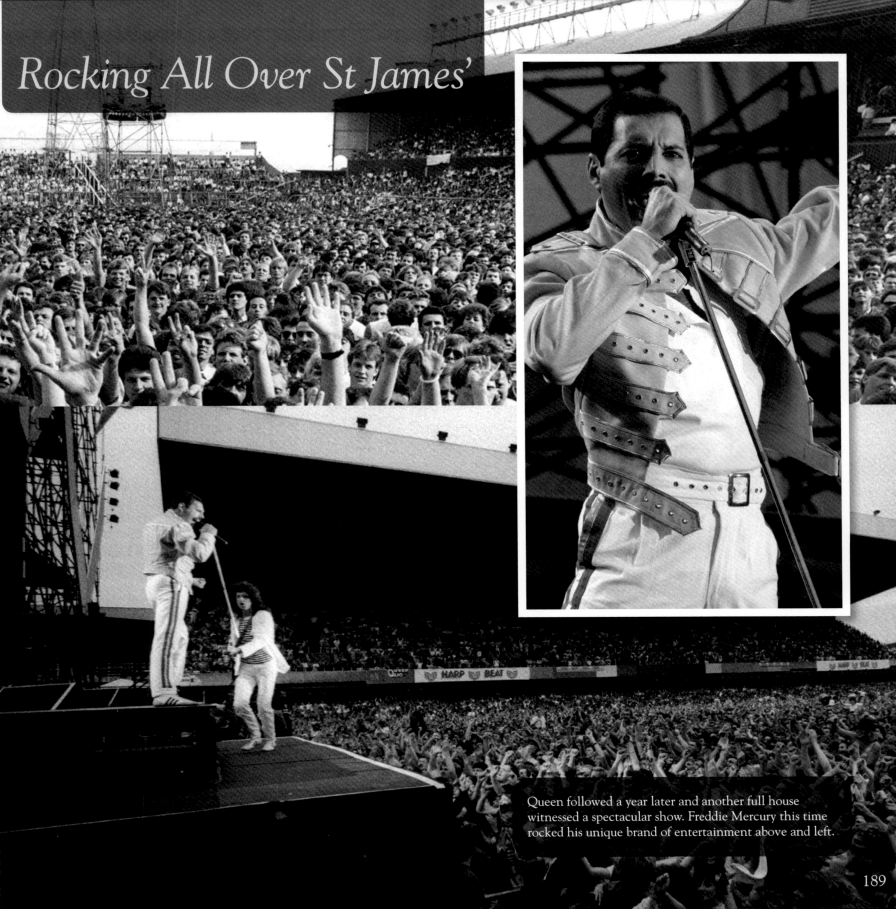

Queen followed a year later and another full house witnessed a spectacular show. Freddie Mercury this time rocked his unique brand of entertainment above and left.

The Boy from Brazil

In a bid to stem mounting criticism following sales of stars Chris Waddle and Peter Beardsl[e]United created headlines by bringing the ver first Brazilian international to the top flight of the English game. The diminutive striker Mirandinha – full name Francisco Ernandi L[i]da Silva – joined the Magpies in August 198[7]a £575,000 fee. United's black-and-white arm[y]of fans turned into a samba army of sombreros and Brazilian flags. Mirandinha showed flashe[s]of brilliance at times, but he never fitted in to what was a struggling line-up that eventually v[as]relegated without much of a fight. He departe[d]soon afterwards.

Mirandinha made headlines scoring for Brazil against England in 1987. McFaul moved quickly to bring him to Tyneside.

> *He was so greedy with the ball that you needed two balls on the pitch – one for him and one for the rest of the team.*
>
> John Hendrie

Manager Willie McFaul (left) with his Brazilian star – a player who United's boss hoped would lead to a Magpie surge up the table.

During this era both supporters and players endured a seemingly never-ending revolving-door to the United manager's office. Jack Charlton walked out after a year in charge and in 1985 the club turned to former goalkeeper Willie McFaul, then on the coaching staff. More changes were to follow in the coming years. Players had to get used to the upheaval. Left to right: David McCreery, Neil McDonald, Peter Jackson, Martin Thomas and Paul Stephenson.

–LEGENDS–

Paul Gascoigne

A dazzling talent unveiled

When Paul Gascoigne helped win the FA Youth Cup for United everyone could see he was a star in the making. As a teenager the somewhat boisterous and jovial Geordie was quickly a regular in the black-and-white line-up, even then showing all the talent, skill and showmanship that was to be a feature of his career. Gazza matured into a match-winning midfielder with vision to create an opening, with skill to make the difference and go past defenders as well as the ability to strike the ball into the net. Sadly, his very best years were not seen at Gallowgate, but at White Hart Lane, in Rome with Lazio and at Ibrox.

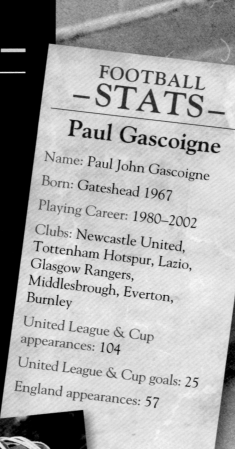

FOOTBALL –STATS–

Paul Gascoigne

Name: Paul John Gascoigne

Born: Gateshead 1967

Playing Career: 1980–2002

Clubs: Newcastle United, Tottenham Hotspur, Lazio, Glasgow Rangers, Middlesbrough, Everton, Burnley

United League & Cup appearances: 104

United League & Cup goals: 25

England appearances: 57

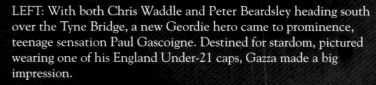

Sweet Temptation

LEFT: With both Chris Waddle and Peter Beardsley heading south over the Tyne Bridge, a new Geordie hero came to prominence, teenage sensation Paul Gascoigne. Destined for stardom, pictured wearing one of his England Under-21 caps, Gazza made a big impression.

ABOVE: He may have been "Daft as a Brush", but Gazza was brilliant with it and soon became the country's hottest property.

RIGHT: Gascoigne had fabulous all-round ability and panache, could strike the ball sweetly and also had the skills to go round opponents – as he does against Liverpool's Mark Lawrenson and Steve Nichol.

FAR RIGHT: The iconic image of the Eighties. A _Daily Mirror_ photographer captures the very moment in February 1988 when Wimbledon's Vinnie Jones gives Gazza something to shout about!

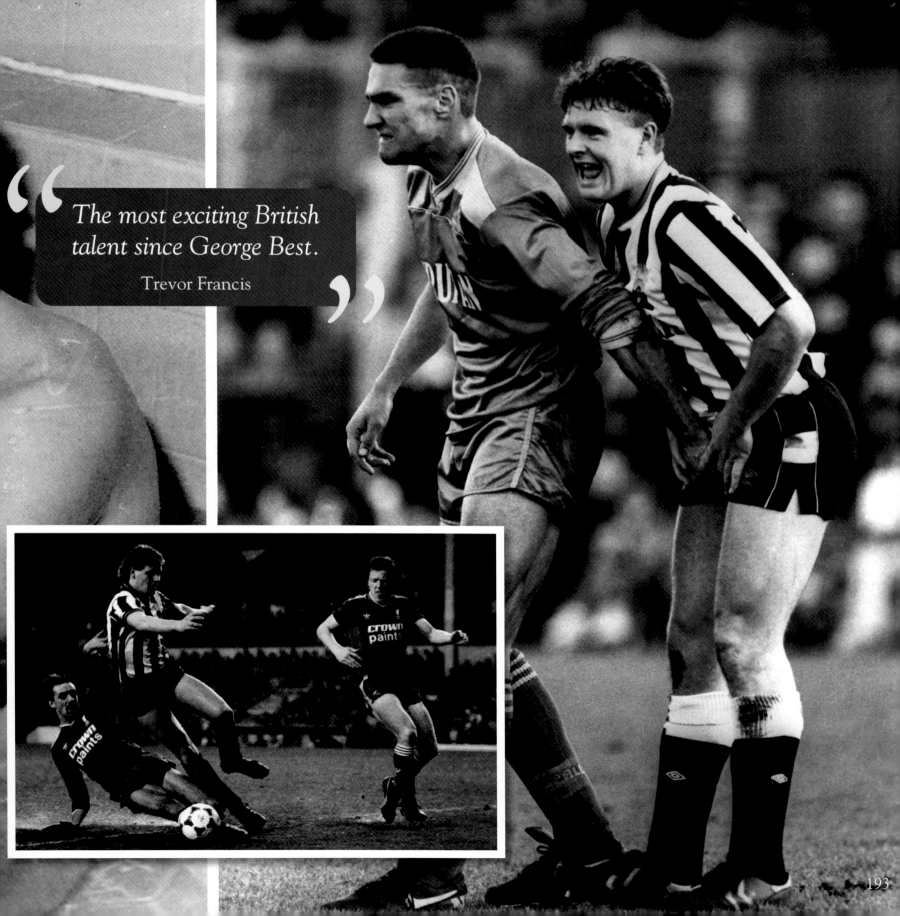

> *The most exciting British talent since George Best.*
>
> Trevor Francis

The Bald Eagle Has Landed

RIGHT: Despite the exceptional talent of Gazza, who was to follow Waddle and Beardsley out of St James' Park, Willie McFaul's team slumped badly in 1988/9 and faced another period in the second tier of football. It was now Jim Smith's turn at the helm, the Bald Eagle taking charge in December 1988.

And Signs Scotland's Skipper

Ossie's Dream-team

LEFT: Scotland captain Roy Aitken was a big-name signing early in 1990. The former Celtic stalwart possessed a formidable track record north of the border and was prominent as United pushed for a quick return to the First Division. However, the Magpies fell in the play-offs – to Sunderland of all clubs – and Smith could no longer take the pressure of managing what was fast becoming the unmanageable. It was all change once more at St James' Park.

BACKGROUND: Newcastle United's fifth boss in just over ten years, Ossie Ardiles was another celebrated personality and another World Cup winner. Appointed in March 1991 and new to the manager's chair with only limited experience at Swindon Town, Ossie had a dream of building a United side based on youth. Out went experienced players, in came raw talent. The outcome was predicable – a slide down the table. Here the Argentinean peers through the fog against Bournemouth during a

Conflict in Toon

By the end of the 1980s Newcastle United's continued mediocrity in the football world – languishing in the second level – was the focus of a rebellion against the ownership of the club. For generations the Board of Directors was a closed shop and the share ownership was contained in the hands of families and friends, many descended from United's origins on Victorian Tyneside. And with the emergence of big money into the game, something had to change in the hot-spot that was St James' Park. The Magpie Group was formed to create that change, to challenge the somewhat antiquated ownership and a bitter share-war for control of the Black 'n' Whites raged for the next three years and more. Huge sums of money exchanged hands for the limited and now valuable share certificates. John Hall (later Sir John) led the crusade, and with his financial backing eventually completed a full-blown takeover of the club. By the time the Premiership had been formed for the 1992/3 season, Newcastle United were ready to be dramatically transformed and join the new, modern elite.

The Pied Piper
Calls the Tune

TOP LEFT: With the club in desperate need of an injection of substantial funds, Chairman Gordon McKeag is pictured at the launch of a share issue in 1990. Unfortunately the initiative flopped badly.

LEFT: Long-serving Club Secretary Russell Cushing (right) had to grapple with a share war for control of United and was caught between the two warring factions. John Hall (left) led the Magpie Group against the existing McKeag regime. It was the start of an intriguing soap-opera on Tyneside to run for 20 years – and keep running!

BACKGROUND: With Ardiles taking United nowhere fast – indeed into the Third Division if anywhere – as John Hall won the power battle, changes were inevitable. The club's new ownership acted swiftly and in February 1992 brought back Kevin Keegan as a talisman in a bid to inspire all – and save the club from the catastrophe of Division Three.

> "You can still break out in a cold sweat when you consider how close we came to relegation."
>
> Kevin Keegan

There was a real risk that the famous Magpies would tumble into the third level of English football for the very first time. In the remaining games of the 1991/2 season, Keegan had one task – to save United from relegation. He did it by a whisker and it was Gavin Peacock (pictured) whose performance at Leicester on the final day of the season ensured safety.

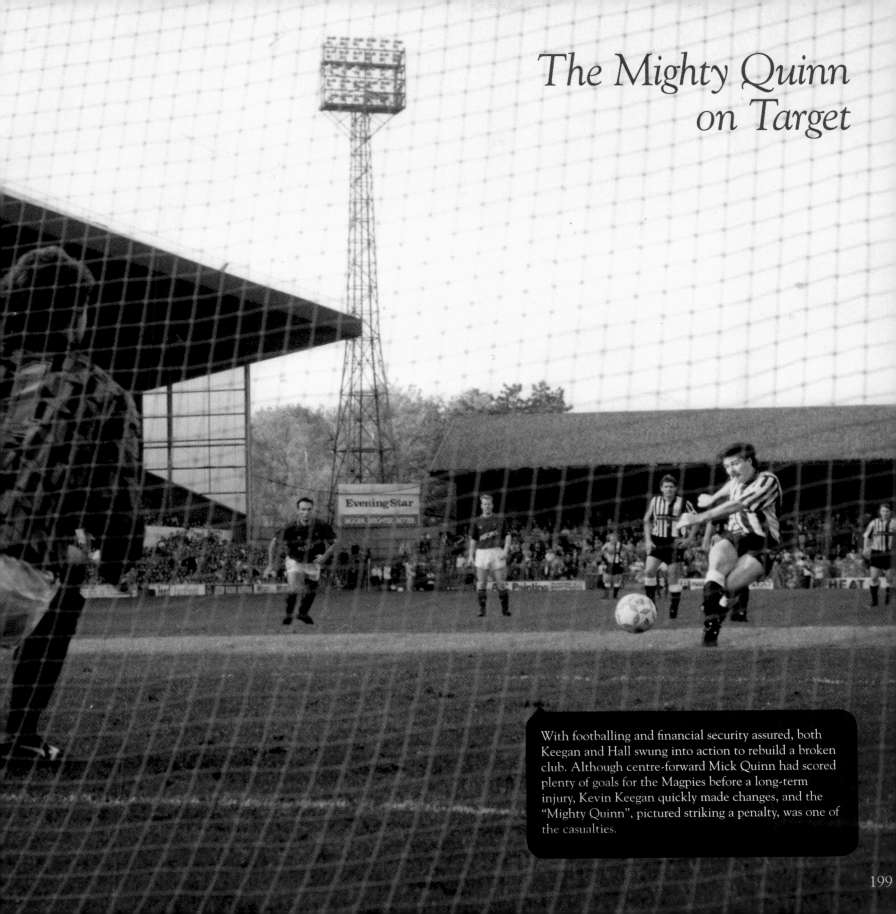

The Mighty Quinn on Target

With footballing and financial security assured, both Keegan and Hall swung into action to rebuild a broken club. Although centre-forward Mick Quinn had scored plenty of goals for the Magpies before a long-term injury, Kevin Keegan quickly made changes, and the "Mighty Quinn", pictured striking a penalty, was one of the casualties.

The Toon Army Arrives

Newcastle United's band of supporters have long been admired; a fanatical, loyal and raucous mass of black and white who have given the side inspiration for generations. Now they are known throughout football as the "Toon Army", yet that title is a modern invention. The club's dedicated fans were branded with the label as the Magpies rebirth began when they entered the Premiership in 1993. A Geordie expression for the town-centre, or Newcastle, Toon evolved into Toon Army. And every Geordie is proud to display the uniform of black-and-white stripes, now very much a tribal identity for the region.

"Newcastle United do have, beyond question, the most loyal fans in football."

Kevin Keegan

The Entertainers Arrive on Stage

Promotion 1993

With the St James' Park revolution in full swing, Kevin Keegan's revamped Magpie side had few notable rivals in the 1992/3 promotion campaign. Creating a record of 11 straight wins from the start of the season, the Magpies cruised to the Football League title in an entertaining and magical manner; with goals galore and sparkling football the order of the day. A win at Grimsby secured top-level football again, while the season was capped with a special 7-1 victory over Leicester on the final day of the season – with United 6-0 up at half-time!

Record: P46 W29 D9 L8 F92 A38 – 96 Pts – Position 1st.
Regular side: Srnicek, Venison, Howey, Scott, Beresford, Lee, Bracewell or O'Brien, Clark, Sheedy or Sellars, Kelly, Cole or Peacock.
Top scorers: Kelly 24, Peacock 12, Cole 12.
Captain: Barry Venison.
Manager: Kevin Keegan.

Kevin Keegan's attacking style of football was a treat to watch; quick-passing, fast-flowing, possession football at its very best. And Newcastle's strikers reaped the benefit. David Kelly, in action against Brentford, had a productive season in 1992/3 with 27 goals all told – yet he was to be replaced for the arrival of the Premiership.

Towards the end of the 1992/3 season Keegan began planning for life in the new world that was branded the Premiership. In March 1993 he splashed out £1.75m for the largely unknown England Under-21 striker Andy Cole. What an impact he was to have! Cole was to take the No. 9 shirt and score a record 41 goals for the club in his first full season.

-LEGENDS-

Kevin Keegan

The Messiah revitalizes the Toon

When England skipper Kevin Keegan joined struggling giant Newcastle United in 1982 it was the start of a special relationship few outside Tyneside could comprehend. An inspiration to all, in his final two years as a player, Keegan rallied the club to ensure promotion then returned as a manager in 1992 to again lead the Magpies as United were transformed into a European force. Lifting the Football League crown, he very nearly secured the Premiership title too, all in a style of football celebrated throughout the country.

FOOTBALL
-STATS-

Kevin Keegan

Name: Joseph Kevin Keegan OBE

Born: Armthorpe 1951

Playing Career: 1967–1984

Clubs: Scunthorpe United, Liverpool, SV Hamburg, Southampton, Newcastle United

United League & Cup appearances: 85

United League & Cup goals: 49

Division One champions 1993

England appearances: 63

Elation at Grimsby...

Newcastle sealed promotion with a 2-0 victory on an emotion-filled evening in Grimsby in May 1993. Kevin Keegan is caught at the very moment of success.

A Trophy for Special K

> "There is a passion about Tyneside that only those who have lived there can possibly understand."
>
> Kevin Keegan

LEFT: Thumbs up from Kevin Keegan as United seal promotion and the Championship trophy. The victors received a magnificent Toon Army welcome home. He very nearly followed that success with the ultimate prize – Premiership silverware.

Toon Support

Since the beginning of the 20th century, Newcastle United have always enjoyed a huge and wonderful support, the envy of most clubs around the country. Gates of 50,000 and over were often to be seen during pre-war years, and while the post-war boom saw attendances soar around the country, they did so nowhere more than at St James' Park. In the 1947/8 season the majestic Toon support created a new average record of over 56,000 at each home fixture. In modern-day football only Manchester United and latterly Arsenal have bettered the Magpies' average for Premier League fixtures. Since the club's stadium enlargement in 2000, Newcastle's average for Premier League action is an impressive 51,000 plus, just about fully 98 per cent capacity. Considering the lack of recent success witnessed on Tyneside, the region certainly deserves its "Hotbed of Football" tag.

From this...

To this...

While Kevin Keegan did the business on the pitch, the Hall regime transformed the club behind the scenes, including developing, at long last, St James' Park. The arena, pictured in 1975, needed to become an all-seater stadium for the 21st century.

By the time Newcastle had become established as a new force in the Premiership, St James' Park had been turned into a wonderful venue to both play and watch football. It was a fortress to the Magpies and created a special atmosphere. Further redevelopment took place in 2000 to increase capacity to over 52,000.